God's Lineup

Testimonies of Major League Baseball Players

God's Lineup

Testimonies of Major League Baseball Players

Kevin & Elizabeth Morrisey

AMBASSADOR INTERNATIONAL
GREENVILLE, SOUTH CAROLINA & BELFAST, NORTHERN IRELAND

www.ambassador-international.com

God's Lineup
Testimonies of Major League Baseball Players

© 2012 by Kevin & Elizabeth Morrisey

Printed in the United States of America

ISBN: 9781935507666

Authors Photo by Paul Wilson
Cover Photos by Elizabeth Morrisey
Cover Design by David Siglin and Matthew Mulder
Page Layout by David Siglin and Matthew Mulder

AMBASSADOR INTERNATIONAL
Emerald House
427 Wade Hampton Blvd.
Greenville, SC 29609, USA
www.ambassador-international.com

AMBASSADOR BOOKS
The Mount
2 Woodstock Link
Belfast, BT6 8DD, Northern Ireland, UK
www.ambassador-international.com

The colophon is a trademark of Ambassador

Now to him who is able to do immeasurably more than all we ask or imagine, according to his power that is at work within us, to him be glory in the church and in Christ Jesus throughout all generations, for ever and ever! Amen.

–Ephesians 3:20-21

Contents

Acknowledgements

I GREW UP IN THE Ozarks of Missouri. During my childhood, attending a St. Louis Cardinals game became a tradition, as well as a family reunion of sorts. Each summer the call went out to the brothers, cousins, aunts, uncles, parents and friends to gather for a game one mid-summer evening.

The summer of 2006 was no different; we rallied the family and met for a Cardinals game in July. However, the Lord had something a little different in mind this time. After the game ended, the family was packing up to head out. My wife, my parents and I noticed a group forming to one side of the stadium. Being curious, we wandered over. We found out it was Family Christian Day at the ballpark. We stayed to hear the players give their testimonies and how Jesus has been working in their lives. After the players had spoken about their faith, an opportunity was given for people to pray and accept Jesus as their Lord and Savior. Several people around me stood up after saying the prayer to indicate they had done this.

Looking around, I saw that the Lord had used the words from a few men who surrendered their lives to Jesus and had the courage to share their testimonies to lead others to a life of salvation. As time passed, this memory stuck with me and I knew the Lord was pressing me to write a book on the testimonies of baseball players.

While I was recording their testimonies and writing the book, the players I interviewed encouraged me continuously. They pushed me to focus the book on Christ and to present the Gospel and the Word because Jesus is the One they look to—the only One who can save us. They know what changes lives is not their words, but the Word of God. This book is about the Lord, and the players kindly donated their time and testimonies to me.

I would like to thank my wife Liz for using her gift of writing from the Lord to pull these testimonies together. I also would like to thank each player and their families for their help, for believing in me, and for being "strong and courageous" Christians.

Above all, this book could not have happened if it were not for the Lord Jesus Christ. I give Him all the praise and thank Him for continuously loving me.

Thank you and Love,
Kevin Morrisey

Let the peace of Christ rule in your hearts
—Colossians 3:15a

Foreword

IN A MINISTRY LIKE BASEBALL Chapel, we have the privilege of bringing God's Word into the ballpark to minister to players, coaches, umpires and everyone connected with the game of baseball. We see lives change every day. Most fans are not aware that there are hundreds of baseball players who are followers of Jesus, and they are surprised to learn that there are chapel services at every ballpark each Sunday and Bible studies during the week.

The stories of faith compiled by Kevin and Elizabeth Morrisey in the following pages represent dozens of lives changed by the power of Jesus Christ. The men featured are not any different than millions of others who have acknowledged their need for a savior and placed their faith in Christ for their salvation. These men just all happen to play professional baseball. Some names are familiar to you, while others are not, but the experiences they share are common to people in all walks of life, including dealing with disappointment, struggles in their marriage, health issues, and coping with death.

Perhaps you picked up this book because you love baseball and want to know more about some of the players who profess Jesus Christ as their Savior. Perhaps you are a young person who plays baseball in your town, or maybe you work in a factory, or you could be retired and trying to enjoy your golden years. Whatever stage of life you are in, you can relate to these stories. As you read, remember that each man talks about the love of God and His offer of the free gift of salvation, not about his own goodness.

It is my hope that as you read these stories, you will sense the power of God that can change your life if you seek Him. For those of you who already have the joy of knowing Christ, may this encourage and strengthen your walk with Him. For those of you who really aren't sure about where you stand with God, I pray that your heart will search for the same thing the men featured in these pages discovered at one point in their lives–that Jesus Christ is truly the way, the truth and the life.

God bless you.
Vince Nauss, President, Baseball Chapel
www.baseballchapel.org

Preface

JESUS CAME TO SAVE US from our sins. He came into the world as a baby and experienced life as a human in order to feel what we feel and to experience what we experience. He left His throne in the Kingdom of Heaven to serve us. He is a great teacher, leader, and healer, but above all he is our Father, our King and our Savior.

Jesus was crucified on the cross, not by Roman soldiers, but *by* us–and *for* us. He did this for us to save us from our sins. No one can earn salvation. There is nothing we can do good enough to earn eternal life. The Lord knows this, and He knows that our sins have created a separation between us and Him. That is why He sent His only son, Jesus, to die for our sins, to defeat Satan, to rise from the grave and to ascend into heaven. The Lord requires us to do only one thing to have salvation. He calls us to believe in Jesus and accept Him as our Lord and Savior.

Those who have accepted Jesus as Lord and Savior–Christians–are saved from their sins, but that does not make them perfect. In fact, while on this earth, we are far from perfect. Each day we must pick up our cross and serve the Lord. Our faith in Jesus can carry us to many places and allow us to have many experiences in our lifetime. A select few have had the blessing to play professional baseball. They have responded to God's calling by recognizing the gifts that they have been given. These players have discovered that their talents and abilities did not take them to pro ball, but the Lord led them there. They have recognized that Major League Baseball is a platform the Lord has given them to share their testimonies and spread the word about Jesus.

Like Paul, these players have chosen not to put their confidence in themselves, in the flesh, or in something worldly. They have chosen to put their confidence in the Lord Jesus Christ.

But whatever was to my profit I now consider loss for the sake of Christ. What is more, I consider everything a loss compared to the surpassing greatness of knowing Christ Jesus my Lord, for whose sake I have lost all things. I consider them rubbish, that I may gain Christ and be found in him, not having a righteousness of my own that comes from the law, but that which is through faith in Christ—the righteousness that comes from God and is by faith. I want to know Christ and the power of his resurrection and the fellowship of sharing in his sufferings, becoming like him in his death, and so, somehow, to attain to the resurrection from the dead.

–Philippians 3:7-11

"God wants to utilize us if we
humble ourselves to Him."
—Tim Drew

Tim Drew

TIMOTHY ANDREW DREW

BORN: August 31, 1978 in Valdosta, GA
FAVORITE BIBLE VERSES: Romans 10:9, Romans 8:31, and Joshua 1:9
SAVED: 9 years old
POSITION: Pitcher
SCHOOL: Lowndes High School in Valdosta, Georgia
DRAFTED: 1st Round of 1997 draft by Cleveland Indians
DEBUT: May 24, 2000 for Cleveland Indians
SEASONS: 2000 – 2004 (Retired)
TEAMS: Indians, Expos, and Braves
NUMBERS: 47, 46

What, then, shall we say in response to this? If God is for us, who can be against us?
—Romans 8:31

It is our responsibility to be obedient to Jesus. We have been given commands from the Lord on loving others and on how to act. When the Lord gives us direction on what He wants, whether through the Holy Bible or through the Holy Spirit, we are to obey. In doing so, we show our love for the Lord.

And this is love: that we walk in obedience to his commands.
—2 John 1:6a

Years	2000-2004	L	4	ER	66
G	35	SV	2	HR	16
GS	11	IP	84.2	BB	39
ERA	7.02	H	113	SO	40
W	2	R	82		

Obedience

Tim Drew

GOD SHOWED UP ONE DAY and knocked his socks off. At least that's the way retired pitcher Tim Drew likes to describe it. He was about twenty when God radically changed him. He began seeing God in a new light and wanted to have a relationship with Him that was deeper and more meaningful.

"I had a desire to grow and understand His will for my life instead of focusing on making money in the big leagues," Drew said. He accepted Christ when he was nine years old and memorized several Scriptures such as Romans 8:31 and Joshua 1:9. So he wouldn't forget them, he pulled the blinds down in his bedroom, got a sharpie pen and wrote those Scriptures on them.

Despite a good start, as he became older he found himself for a period living a life that wasn't committed to Christ. Since God has gotten his attention, Drew strives to become more like Christ. "The Holy Spirit moved in and took control of my life," he said. "Now I'm a husband and father and it's a vital time to live a life of faith. Without it (faith), it's impossible to please God."

Drew compares his life playing baseball and moving around to a rollercoaster. He also suffered a setback in 2005 when he injured his shoulder. He explained, "There was always the uncertainty of going to a new team. If you don't have Christ, I don't know how you make it through those times. In ten years, I moved fifty plus times, but it was my faith in Christ that carried me through the nights that I would be crying in my room because I didn't understand."

God rattled him again during his second Major League start. He took the mound and noticed that he was the only one on the ball field who wasn't an all-star. "I kept verses under my hat. The first ones were Romans 8:31, Joshua 1:9 and Colossians 3:23. I said to the pitching coach 'when God wants me to pitch well in the big leagues I will.' I was in Montreal and I pitched great. When God says it's time; it's time. All good things come from above."

Drew began sharing his faith with others. "I was working with Baseball Chapel and out of the blue a player wanted to give his life to Jesus. I was with him all season long. I was fortunate to see a lot of guys that I knew come to Christ when I played."

He is thankful that God has given him the ability to freely communicate his faith to others. "I'm a person that takes a leadership role. I thank God he opened the door for me to have some credibility to speak to people and to have them listen. I have the ability to love people. I say this humbly because the fruits of the spirit have worked in my life. God wants to utilize us if we humble ourselves to Him."

"People are always watching whether you're a Major League pitcher or someone else," Drew said. He believes that what you do for your family, friends and your hometown are the most important things you will ever do.

The word of God will change a person's life, he said. "I challenge those who read this book that they discover who Christ is…. It's about asking 'Who is God?' God shows up and He'll knock your socks off. That's what He did in my life."

"Much has been given and much has been expected. Not just in a material sense but also in a spiritual sense. God has revealed Himself to us and proved faithful. What are we to do with that?"
—Scott Sanderson

Scott Sanderson

SCOTT DOUGLAS SANDERSON

BORN: July 22, 1956 in Dearborn, MI
FAVORITE BIBLE VERSES: Luke 12:48 and Luke 16:10
SAVED: College
POSITION: Pitcher
2011 Team: Baseball Player Agent for Moye Sports Associates
SCHOOL: Vanderbilt University
DRAFTED: 3rd Round of 1977 draft by Montreal Expos
DEBUT: August 6, 1978 for Montreal Expos
SEASONS: 1978 – 1996 (Retired)
TEAMS: Expos, Cubs, Yankees, Athletics, Giants, White Sox, and Angels
NUMBERS: 40, 21, 24, 22, 29
ACCOMPLISHMENTS: All-Star Selection 1991

Whoever can be trusted with very little can also be trusted with much, and whoever is dishonest with very little will also be dishonest with much.
—Luke 16:10

Have you ever played the game "Trust" where you fall back and are caught by your friend? Well, Jesus never misses. He will always catch you. What amazing trust you can have in the Lord, having that knowledge. As the Lord's children we have been trusted with many gifts. Jesus has given us time, money, and skills. He trusts that we will use His gifts for His glory. When we do use His gifts for His glory, we earn the Lord's trust and He will give us more.

From everyone who has been given much, much will be demanded; and from the one who has been entrusted with much, much more will be asked.
—Luke 12:48

Years	1978-1996	L	143	ER	1093
G	472	SV	5	HR	297
GS	407	IP	2561.2	BB	625
ERA	3.84	H	2590	SO	1611
W	163	R	1209		

Trust

WE HAVE A TENDENCY TO ask the question "Why me?" at the wrong time, according to Scott Sanderson. Why do we never ask it when things are going well, and not just when they are going badly? "(These) … are really good questions to ask," Sanderson said. "I just think that we should be asking them when our plate is full and things are going good. We have a tendency to overlook it."

It was early in his faith that Sanderson began asking himself: *Why do I have all that I have? Why have I been afforded such an incredibly great life?* "It was a head scratcher to me why was I afforded these luxuries and so many aren't," he said. "I've been blessed for a long time now, and I don't want to lose sight of the fact that God wants me to do something with that rather than it just be for my own pleasure."

Sanderson was a freshman in college when he began to open his heart to having a personal relationship with Jesus. "I wanted to learn and grow. I was interested and hungry but young on a maturity level," he said.

Soon he was drafted to play ball for the Montreal Expos and found that he wanted everyone to like him. He would act one way with one group of guys and another with a different group. "I found out it was not the way to go about things at all." When a teammate said to him "I'm trying to figure out who you are," the comment was convicting for Sanderson. "I realized that was a great point he was making. At that point I decided the right thing to do is put a stake in the ground and say, 'This is who I am, this is what I believe and this is how I'm going to act.'" Sanderson said he's trying to do it in a way that shows God's love but is determined not to be wishy-washy about what he stands for.

One thing that helped him throughout his career was the fact that he was fortunate to have some Christian teammates and friends. "It's easier to take a stance and do the right thing when you have other people that are there next to you, encouraging you and trying to do the same thing," he said. "I had people encouraging me and lifting me up. Christian fellowship is such a powerful force."

Sanderson wants to shine in a way that glorifies the Lord. Matthew 5:14-16 talks about that subject. *"You are the light of the world. A city on a hill cannot be hidden. Neither do people light a lamp and put it under a bowl. Instead they put it on its stand, and it gives light to everyone in the house. In the same way, let your light shine before others, that they may see your good deeds and glorify your Father in heaven."*

"We have a tendency that we want to shine in a way that we get the glory," Sanderson said. "My desire is not that I would shine but that Christ would shine through me. And if there is anything I do that is worth recognition in any way, it's not me who gets the recognition but God."

He believes one of our biggest lessons in life is when we realize that we can't do anything by our own power. "We absolutely have to put our faith in Christ. Sometimes we just have to get to a point where God is the only one we can trust. When He shows Himself in a big way, how can you possibly ignore that?"

"In an everyday practical sense, the Gospel was sustaining me through times of difficulty whether baseball my first year at Alabama or when my wife was sick with cancer. It was the sustaining faith that got me through those difficult times, also seeing that was part of God's plan."
—Andy Phillips

Andy Phillips

GEORGE ANDREW PHILLIPS

BORN: April 6, 1977 in Tuscaloosa, AL

FAVORITE BIBLE VERSES: Psalm 27

SAVED: 7 years old

POSITION: First Base

2011 Team: Assistant Baseball Coach for the University of Alabama

SCHOOL: University of Alabama

DRAFTED: 7th Round of 1999 draft by New York Yankees

DEBUT: September 14, 2004 for New York Yankees

SEASONS: 2004 – 2008 (Retired)

TEAMS: Yankees, Reds, and Mets

NUMBERS: 39, 14, 18, 12, 29, 46

The Lord is my light and my salvation—whom shall I fear? The Lord is the stronghold of my life—of whom shall I be afraid?
—Psalm 27:1

Jesus is the Lord of generations. He has been here since the beginning of time and will be here throughout eternity. He being here shows the sustaining strength and love He has for us. The Lord will never abandon us in times of difficulty, hurt and despair. The Lord feels and experiences what we feel and experience. We just need to keep our faith in Him.

The Son is the radiance of God's glory and the exact representation of his being, sustaining all things by his powerful word.
—Hebrews 1:3a

Years	2004-2008	H	139	SB	3
G	259	2B	25	CS	5
PA	604	3B	4	BB	34
AB	557	HR	14	SO	110
R	77	RBI	70	BA	.250

Sustaining

Andy Phillips

WHEN GOING THROUGH SOME OF his darkest hours, Andy Phillips knew he had to fully surrender everything to Jesus. In a moment's notice in 2006 he and his wife's lives were turned upside down when she suffered a miscarriage and was diagnosed with a rare form of cancer.

"I was searching and living in the Scriptures," he said, adding that he found himself receiving strength through the passages in Psalms. "I was reading about what God says about His faithfulness. I had an understanding that regardless of the outcome I had to trust in Him. There was nothing I could do to change the situation, and it became a moment of true surrender."

God was good and soon blessed them with a child. "It was a very rewarding time to see God sustain you through something you never thought you'd make it through," Phillips said. "We had to embrace the path God chose for us. Scripture says 'in all things God works for the good of those who love Him.'"

As a young child, Phillips began to understand the good news of Jesus while watching a cartoon portraying Donald Duck as Scrooge. "I saw the reality of eternity," he said. His faith remained strong by having a family that regularly was involved with church.

Phillips realizes that God had a plan to work in his life through the sport of baseball. "When you put on a baseball uniform, it automatically opens up opportunities to be involved in people's lives," he said. "I've been able to share the Gospel with people on an everyday basis."

Phillip's dark times have helped him to give hope to people who are also walking through difficulties. "It's amazing to see how God has used that situation to encourage people in their situations and encourage them in the Lord."

While Phillips played baseball in Japan for two years, he was challenged spiritually. "When you're in a place where there is nothing (Christian) and it's just you, God and the Bible and that's all you have to lean on, you realize that it's His word that we should worship and follow," he said. "Whether we have church, Baseball Chapel or other ministries, we have to be careful those things don't become what we worship. You (come to) see how dependent you were on other things. It's almost a reality check that the things you serve should be for Christ."

He now understands the importance of developing a true relationship with Christ and being grounded in the Word of God. "Ultimately that's why Scripture teaches so much about the Word and the importance for us to establish time alone in the Word and in prayer," he said. "When you get to the point where that is all you have, it exposes what your relationship is all about."

"When we face those hardships, the sin and struggles in our life, we already have victory through the shed blood of Christ. We have all the power we need to live a God-honoring life."
—Ben Zobrist

Ben Zobrist

BENJAMIN THOMAS ZOBRIST

BORN: May 26, 1981 in Eureka, IL

FAVORITE BIBLE VERSES: Galatians 2:20

SAVED: 12 or 13 years old

POSITIONS: Right Field, Second Base, and Shortstop

2011 TEAM: Tampa Bay Rays

SCHOOLS: Dallas Baptist University and Olivet Nazarene University

DRAFTED: 6th Round of 2004 draft by Houston Astros

DEBUT: August 1, 2006 for Tampa Bay Devil Rays

SEASONS: 2006 – 2011 (Active)

TEAMS: Devil Rays and Rays

NUMBER: 18

ACCOMPLISHMENTS: All Star Selection—2009

I have been crucified with Christ and I no longer live, but Christ lives in me. The life I live in the body, I live by faith in the Son of God, who loved me and gave himself for me.
—Galatians 2:20

The Lord calls us to have faith—faith in Jesus, faith in the Holy Spirit, and faith in the power of the Lord. Through our faith there is nothing impossible. In Matthew 17:20, Jesus tells us that if we have faith as small as a mustard seed, we can move mountains. The mountains are the obstacles that we face each and every day in our lives, and through the Lord we can overcome them.

Now faith is being sure of what we hope for and certain of what we do not see.
—Hebrews 11:1

Years	2006-2011	H	542	SB	67
G	604	2B	120	CS	18
PA	2458	3B	19	BB	298
AB	2108	HR	72	SO	423
R	317	RBI	314	BA	.257

Faith

Ben Zobrist

WORRY, FEAR AND DEPRESSION BEGAN to take hold of Ben Zobrist, but once he devoted his life to the Lord things began to change.

Zobrist was first introduced to Christ as a young child. He understood that he was a sinner and didn't want to go to hell but wanted to spend eternity in heaven. "I remember spending time reading the Bible and trying to read through it all in one year. I tried to be obedient to God and my parents in my childhood."

As he got older, sports became an idol in his life. "Everything about my sport was what I was all about. The Lord got a hold of my heart to show me I had other things that were taking (His) place on the throne of my life."

Zobrist was unsure about his future after high school but knew he needed to be dependent on Christ for everything. "I realized how much I needed the Lord and really turned everything over to Him," he said. "I started walking with Him, being obedient and more in tune with the Spirit and what He wanted to do in my life."

Baseball began to be a serious part of his life in college, and he was offered a full ride to Olivet Nazarene University. "God opened the door to go to a Christian school and play ball."

In 2006, Zobrist made it to the Major Leagues, but he still wasn't immune to struggles. He continued to do well but was injured and worked hard to stay in the big leagues.

He was soon sent back down to the Minors. "I hit spiritual doubt and wondered what I was supposed to be doing," he said. "Instead of trusting in the Lord, I became depressed, anxious and worried. Through that time, the Lord made Himself even more real."

Zobrist has learned lessons from the ups and downs of his career: "God wants to change our hearts, and His success is not the same as worldly success. It is more about what is going on in your heart, not in your circumstances. Our delight should be in Him and His eternal promises rather than on worldly success on a ball field."

God was faithful and gave him strength while he recovered from injuries. In 2008 his team the Tampa Bay Rays, made it to the playoffs. And in 2009 Zobrist was an All Star. As a professional athlete, Zobrist understands the need to depend on the Lord and to be more of a godly man.

"In baseball, people are watching you and your every move. I've heard negative comments about how I live my faith out loud…to really speak the truth to people." Zobrist believes if we stand up for Christ and live a life Christ is going to be honored by, then our lives will be blessed.

Zobrist is concerned about today's culture and the idolizing of professional athletes. "It's a real epidemic that, rather than spending time on Christ, we are spending time on loving sports and loving athletes. If I could say one thing to the kids or fans, it's don't settle for less than the best. We settle for less than perfect and we had perfect at our fingertips. You hear about it in Scripture and the Gospel and His name is Jesus. Why do we spend so much money, time and effort on all these worldly pursuits when He is the best thing that there is?"

The year 2010 was a test of perseverance for Zobrist as he struggled all year to find his groove. "He's filling up the rocky soil still in my spirit, but He's gracious and loving," Zobrist said. "I owe everything in my life to Christ because I would have nothing without Him."

"The World and Satan want us to live in fear—fear of what this person says, fear of what might happen, fear of what if we are found out. We are constantly bombarded by fear, and we live in bondage to it."
—Greg McMichael

Greg McMichael

GREGORY WINSTON MCMICHAEL

BORN: December 1, 1966 in Knoxville, TN

FAVORITE BIBLE VERSES: 2 Timothy 1:7

SAVED: 8th Grade

POSITIONS: Pitcher

2011 TEAM: MLBA Consulting LLC Senior Advisor for Alumni Relations to the Atlanta Braves

SCHOOL: University of Tennessee

DRAFTED: 7th Round of 1988 draft by Cleveland Indians

DEBUT: April 12, 1993 for Atlanta Braves

SEASONS: 1993 – 2000 (Retired)

TEAMS: Braves, Mets, Athletics, and Dodgers

NUMBERS: 38, 36, 35, 49

ACCOMPLISHMENTS: World Series Champions 1995

For God did not give us a spirit of timidity, but a spirit of power, of love and of self-discipline.
—2 Timothy 1:7

The war we are fighting is against Satan and sin. This is a war that we have to fight each and every day. At times Satan appears to be strong, attacking us constantly. As Christians, we should put our armor on each day for the war because we love the Lord. We can take joy and comfort that we are not fighting alone. The Lord is with us on the battlefield leading the charge. The amazing thing is that we have already won—through Jesus and His power!

Years	1993-2000	L	29	ER	189
G	453	SV	53	HR	42
GS	0	IP	523.1	BB	193
ERA	3.25	H	483	SO	459
W	31	R	215		

Power

Greg McMichael

GREG MCMICHAEL USED TO TRY to be fulfilled by trophies and competition. Now he's seeking the Lord to fulfill his life. He wanted to feel good and be told, "job well done" but he soon realized that those things weren't what was important in life.

When he was in 8th grade, McMichael was diagnosed with a rare cartilage disease and was told he would never play sports again. Sports were the one thing he thought was important in his life. "I remember crying, knowing all of my significance was wrapped up in those trophies and sports," he said.

To fill that void he began smoking pot, drinking and chasing girls. Through these times of rebellion, he saw changes in his parents' lives. They divorced, accepted Christ and then remarried. "I saw who God was," said McMichael. "I was going through the worst experience, and I saw this unbelievable thing happen to my family, even though I didn't know the significance of it at the time."

As he became stronger, he was determined and played baseball his sophomore year. He did well but continued to have a battle in his head and his heart as God spoke to him through his parents. They shared the Gospel with their son. He knew he was miserable and thought: *Why not accept Him?*

"When you are the life of the party and then change, everyone's expectations are still there. So how do you become a new person without being in bondage to the old person? The fear was very real. I lost friends and people rejected me."

McMichael's perspective on life totally changed: "God renewed me and made me a new person." As he got better and better at playing ball, he received a full ride to Tennessee. But the challenges didn't end there. "By no means was the rest of my life rosy. I continued to have some problems but I got drafted," he said.

McMichael continued to have bumps in the road and his faith was tested. "God took me to depths I never thought He would with the death of (my) son," he said. "There were times I wanted to quit baseball. Life never got any easier. If anything—it got more difficult. But my relationship with the Lord continues to get deeper, and I understand more about what relationships are about."

After retiring from baseball with the Atlanta Braves, he tried to run his own business but he wasn't as successful as he thought he would be. "You come out as a successful athlete and you think 'whatever I do, I will be successful.' But I was just a rookie. I needed a mentor and coach but I was too prideful to realize that."

"I had to look in the mirror and say, 'God who am I? What am I doing?' All that stuff from the past—the shame and pain of looking to be fulfilled through a business—all came back up again. God taught me that you're never immune from the old man," he said. "You have to continue to keep short accounts with God and take that old, sinful nature to the cross and confess."

These life challenges seemed negative when McMichael was in the midst of things, but now he can see how God used them in his life. "I'm learning to get in touch with what God desires for me," he said. "My job now is a blessing." McMichael is the MLBA Consulting LLC Senior Advisor for Alumni Relations to the Atlanta Braves.

"I truly believe a lot of baseball players experience their only community in the locker room. And then when they are done playing, they never experience community again," he said. "I'm excited about trying to bring community back in their lives through the alumni association and I have the opportunity to speak into their lives again and love them well. I'm living out of my whole heart."

"I felt called to play baseball and spent a lot of time in the Minor Leagues. I did not know where I was going, but I knew God had begun that work and that I was supposed to play for a reason. I was called to play."
—Matt Diaz

Matt Diaz

MATT EDWARD DIAZ

BORN: March 3, 1978 in Portland, OR
FAVORITE BIBLE VERSES: Philippians 1:6
SAVED: College
POSITIONS: Left Field
2011 TEAM: Pittsburg Pirates and Atlanta Braves
SCHOOL: Florida State University
DRAFTED: 17th Round of 1999 draft by Tampa Bay Devil Rays
DEBUT: July 19, 2003 for Tampa Bay Devil Rays
SEASONS: 2003 – 2011 (Active)
TEAMS: Pirates, Braves, Royals, and Devil Rays
NUMBERS: 25, 34, 23
ACCOMPLISHMENTS: Cofounder of the Diaz Family Foundation

Being confident of this, that he who began a good work in you will carry it on to completion until the day of Christ Jesus.
—Philippians 1:6

At times confidence and cockiness can be mistaken for each other; however, they are quite different. We are called to do everything as if we are doing it for the Lord. Jesus has blessed us each with gifts and talents, and it is our responsibility to recognize them and apply them. Through these gifts we can have the confidence that the Lord is with us. We should ask that His will be done through our gifts and talents and be humbled by the fact that He chose us.

Years	2003-2011	H	519	SB	33
G	675	2B	91	CS	16
PA	1914	3B	14	BB	96
AB	1755	HR	43	SO	354
R	201	RBI	212	BA	.296

Confidence

Matt Diaz

NOTHING WARMS MATT DIAZ'S HEART more than when his two children talk about Jesus. He recalls a time when his two-year-old son was looking down at his own shirt and said that he was looking for Jesus in his heart. Diaz wants his children to know that they were wonderfully made in God's image, and there is a reason for them being here on earth—to further His Kingdom and live out His purpose.

Diaz, who (at the time of this writing) is an outfielder for the Atlanta Braves, isn't shy about being a Christian and looks at baseball more as a purpose and a mission than a game or career. "It's not necessarily to go save every ball player I come in contact with. That's not my job. Jesus did all the saving we need. My job is just to live the life I'm called to live in front of these guys on a daily basis."

During the 2008 season, Diaz tore a ligament in his knee and felt challenged to look back at his walk with Christ. He questioned: *Am I a baseball player who happens to follow Christ or am I a Christian who happens to play baseball?* He could see that God was there through his injury, and it even allowed him to spend some much-needed time with his family. "We just had a new baby. I got to see her and see my family more. I was able to enjoy the extra time with the family and not be wishing I was somewhere else playing baseball and take it for what it was—which was a hidden blessing."

Christianity had always been a part of Diaz's life. He grew up in a Christian home and took the opportunity of an altar call at the age of thirteen to give his life to Christ. However, it wasn't a deep commitment. Diaz was finding his identity in baseball. He did well in high school and was playing on a college summer league in California. It was the first time he had been away from home, not attending church or reading his Bible.

Then the draft came. Diaz wasn't drafted, and it shook his confidence. College opportunities kept falling through left and right until his only option was Florida State University where one of his brothers attended. Although it didn't seem ideal, he can now look back and "see God's hands on the steering wheel of my life. I spent six weeks that summer without time with God, and it left me feeling empty like there had to be something more."

That "something" happened when he finally decided to sit back down with his Bible. That's when he really turned his life over to Christ. "I was in my apartment alone in college and it was the third night there. I was getting into the Word, and everything I read just hit me square between the eyes. I felt Him calling me to make a decision and have a turning point in my life."

Since that decision, one of the many blessings Diaz has had in his life is peace of mind. After his injury he wasn't sure what was going to happen, but he knew who was in control. "That's the biggest blessing I've had in baseball. It's such a game of uncertainty, and I can be certain of one thing, that is that I am not in control and that is a great thought to have. Just let go and know that God *is* in control. I don't know how people make it in baseball because it's so uncertain," he added. "We don't live in reality as baseball players. My relationship with Christ has given me an eternal perspective on this."

Being a baseball player and a Christian can have its challenges. "Just because I'm a Christian doesn't mean I don't have passion for the game and that I'm not going to play aggressively. Unfortunately, that is the reputation Christians have had around baseball for years, so it's kind of a tough reputation to shake."

Seeing life transformations, especially amongst fellow team-mates, makes it all worth it in his eyes. "You see their entire lives turn around," he said. "The most amazing stories I've seen God do in the locker room are (with) the guys you don't expect, guys you would look at and judge and be glad you're not living that life. God goes after those hearts, and those hearts are open to Him. 'Every man knocking at the door of a brothel is looking for Jesus.' It's a crazy quote but it's true."

Diaz doesn't want to be seen as a "Bible Thumper" but just someone who loves Jesus and wants to share Him with others. There are people who walk around quoting Scripture, he explains, "but that's not really how Jesus did it. He just went around loving on people."

Not only is Diaz's faith important to him on the field, it's also important at home. He is married and has three young children. "God is definitely the rock that our family is trying to be built on."

In bringing many sons and daughters to glory, it was fitting that God, for whom and through whom everything exists, should make the pioneer of their salvation perfect through what he suffered.

Hebrews 2:10

"Jesus promises us direction, purpose, and value—great promises for us in (John 14:6) as His children."
—Ricky Horton

Ricky Horton

RICKY NEAL HORTON

BORN: July 30, 1959 in Poughkeepsie, NY
FAVORITE BIBLE VERSES: Proverbs 3:5-6, John 14:6, Genesis 1:1, and Galatians 5:22
SAVED: 22 or 23 years old
POSITIONS: Pitcher
2011 TEAM: Multi-Area Director of the Greater St. Louis FCA and St. Louis Cardinals Broadcaster on FSN Midwest
SCHOOL: University of Virginia
DRAFTED: 4th Round of 1980 draft by St. Louis Cardinals
DEBUT: April 7, 1984 for St. Louis Cardinals
SEASONS: 1984 – 1990 (Retired)
TEAMS: Cardinals, White Sox, and Dodgers
NUMBERS: 49, 26, 29

Jesus answered, "I am the way and the truth and the life. No one comes to the Father except through me."
—John 14:6

When Jesus answered that He is "the way and the truth and the life," He was giving direction to us. The only way to be saved from our sinful lives and to have eternal life in heaven with the Lord is through Jesus. This promise does give us direction, purpose, and value in our time here on earth and that time is meant to be lived for Jesus.

Years	1984-1990	L	27	ER	281
G	325	SV	15	HR	55
GS	53	IP	673.1	BB	222
ERA	3.76	H	696	SO	319
W	32	R	301		

Direction

Ricky Horton

RICKY HORTON HAS PEACE, JOY and patience, and he attributes that to God's work in his life. "It's not about me, but Christ working through me," he said. "I know at a deep level that I have value and joy that I just can't explain."

But it wasn't always like that for Horton. In the past, he thought faith was a weakness. In fact, he used to ridicule his fellow teammates who went to chapel. But when he was a Minor League baseball player in the early 1980s, God began to reveal Himself and convicted Horton of his sins. "God was opening my eyes, and I started to see things differently. I never thought of myself as a bad guy, but on certain levels I was arrogant and selfish. I've become much less sharp-tongued, less self-centered, and I see others' needs in the way God might see their needs." Horton began to read and study the Bible.

Horton, who now oversees the greater St. Louis area for Fellowship of Christian Athletes, grew up with a church background and strong morals. He was baptized and went through confirmation, but faith was not a central part of his family's life. Now he has made sure that God is part of the lives of his family. He has two children attending the University of Missouri and his wife of 26 years leads regular Bible studies. "I don't know how people do it without God's wisdom and direction," he said.

When God first began revealing Himself to Horton, he recalls an incident at a basketball pick-up game. He had been very aggressive toward a fellow player but suddenly stopped dead in his tracks and asked the guy to forgive him. That moment had tremendous meaning for Horton. He knew it was a sign that he needed to change his attitude. "I believe it was God working in my life to convict me of my sin."

Horton can recall other ball players who made a difference in his life. He remembers when Orel Hershiser was pitching; the chaplain would come and pray with him in front of the crowd. "God can work through us when you're hitting 0.190 or throwing 56 innings in a row and not giving up a run like Orel." Another player, John Shelby, would erase his name in the locker room and write Proverbs 3:5-6 instead. "He lived the Christian life and was a great brother and friend."

He urges others to make sure they look at the athlete's testimony and not the athlete. "Don't follow them. Follow Christ," he said. "Don't put all of your faith in Tim Tebow or Albert Pujols because they are just sinful men saved by grace. Put your faith in the One they put their faith in. A testimony isn't about the player, but about God."

Horton feels he's been able to experience Galatians 5:22: "But the fruit of the Spirit is love, joy, peace, patience, kindness, goodness, faithfulness." However it's always a daily struggle to live the Christian life. He said it's a continuous time of attempting to turn away from sin and the evil nature we have in us. "I'm always careful and aspire not to do it again, but it has to do with daily seeking Him and offering (my life) up as a living sacrifice. If I don't do that daily, then I'm open for avenues that I don't want to go down."

"I know we have a belief and promise beyond what the rest of the world does, and it shouldn't surprise me. But it does."

"It's amazing how God works and how He weaves our lives together and, if we are patient and wait, how God keeps stringing His picture together."
—Todd Worrell

Todd Worrell

TODD ROLAND WORRELL

BORN: September 28, 1959 in Arcadia, CA
FAVORITE BIBLE VERSES: Joshua 1:9
SAVED: 10 years old
POSITIONS: Pitcher
2011 TEAM: Pro Ministry Associate of the Greater St. Louis FCA and Owner of Firesteel Creek Hunting Lodge in South Dakota
SCHOOL: Biola University
DRAFTED: 1st Round of 1982 draft by St. Louis Cardinals
DEBUT: August 28, 1985 for St. Louis Cardinals
SEASONS: 1985 – 1997 (Retired)
TEAMS: Cardinals and Dodgers
NUMBER: 38
ACCOMPLISHMENTS: National League Rookie of the Year—1986; All Star Selection—1988, 1995, 1996; National League Rolaids Relief Man of the Year—1986

"Have I not commanded you? Be strong and courageous. Do not be terrified; do not be discouraged, for the LORD your God will be with you wherever you go."
—Joshua 1:9

"Be strong and courageous" is repeated four times in Joshua 1. This was a command that the Lord gave to Joshua prior to leading the Israelites across the Jordan River into the promise land. This same command is repeated eight additional times in the Bible. Jesus calls us to be strong and courageous because He is with us. We will face hard times and we will face persecutions in our life. Not once did the Lord promise we wouldn't. But the Lord promised that He would never leave or forsake us.

Years	1985-1997	L	52	ER	238
G	617	SV	256	HR	65
GS	0	IP	693.2	BB	247
ERA	3.09	H	608	SO	628
W	50	R	264		

Courage

FOR THOSE OF US WHO have accepted Christ as our Lord and Savior, we can usually remember a date and time when it happened. Worrell remembers it clearly. He was watching Billy Graham on television when he was preaching in Los Angeles. Graham had an altar call at the end, and 10-year-old Worrell accepted the Lord. He understood God's love at that age, but as he got older it became even clearer.

"For kids it can be confusing," he said. "I'm not sure if you can see a big change at that time. It has to grow and mature." For Worrell, that came in junior high. "As far as sinking into the heart... when you're older and aware of who you really are and your position to God and sinfulness (is when it can change.) By the time I got into high school, I had a whole different picture of what was expected of a believer than I did when I was ten."

Worrell's youth pastor was a big influence on his life. He was able to stay strong when faced with peer pressures. "You're willing to make that sacrifice because you believe that strongly in your relationship with the Lord. That kind of gelled for me when I was in high school."

Worrell went to college to become a youth pastor, but God had a different plan for his life. He found himself as one of the top ten baseball players in the nation in the early 1980s. It was difficult for him when this sudden fork in the road appeared, but he realized God must be presenting this baseball opportunity for a reason and he didn't want to ignore it. "It's great to get advice and wisdom, but you still have to sit down in a quiet place and make the decision. As I grow in my faith, it's comforting that God says His ways and thoughts are not my ways and thoughts. When I applied that to my situation, it made sense."

As he began his baseball career, Worrell realized he had built a protective fence around himself with church and attending a Christian school. His life was comfortable in his relationship with the Lord; it wasn't being challenged. "If you're not having tension and not dealing with conflict, you have something wrong in your relationship with the Lord. Looking back on it now, God was preparing me for a process down the line."

While in the minors for three years, Worrell struggled with loneliness. He had no friends or family with him. He realized he was being tested as a believer and decided to fight through the loneliness. "It took my rookie season to finally be able to understand that this was part of a process," he said. "There are things we dislike and try to get out of. These are things God is using in your life to shape and mold you and move you forward in the process of where He's trying to get you. I turned to my relationship with the Lord and it helped with the loneliness."

Another turning point for Worrell was when he had "Tommy John" surgery (reconstruction of the elbow) in 1989. He began to question whether he was really serving his career or serving God. "It gave me a pause in life and it couldn't have come at a better time. What God has put in front of me has been for a purpose. And most of that is shaping and molding my relationship with Him."

In spite of his Christian background, Worrell understands the importance of having a connection and relationship with non-believers. "We're not better than them. We've unintentionally elevated ourselves. Non-believers don't understand our relationship with the Lord. We're being viewed as untouchable. I have just as many problems and sin in my life as unbelievers. We want to change them." But he stressed that Jesus didn't approach non-believers like that. "It was about the condition of their heart," he said. "It's a hard thing to get around and understand."

Worrell believes those who are following Jesus need to grasp what their position is relative to God. "We are sinful. Do we really grasp that as believers? It's one of the biggest reasons why Christians get labeled hypocrites. It's not about how you view the world. It's about how the world views you. As believers, we're not really understanding our position."

We just need to embrace and love others for who they are, Worrell said. "It's a privilege to see how God brings change into people's lives. It's not our job. The only power that can change them is the Holy Spirit."

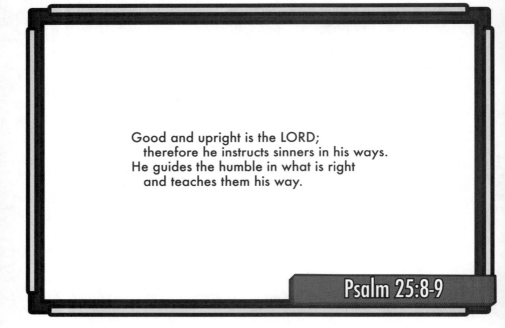

Good and upright is the LORD;
    therefore he instructs sinners in his ways.
He guides the humble in what is right
    and teaches them his way.

Psalm 25:8-9

"I realize I don't want Jesus in my life because of the things I get, I want Jesus in my life. That is the prize. That is what we are striving for. We don't get heaven, we get Jesus, and He happens to be in heaven."
—Steve Sisco

Steven Sisco

STEVEN MICHAEL SISCO

BORN: December 2, 1969 in Thousand Oaks, CA
FAVORITE BIBLE VERSES: Galatians 2:20 and 2 Timothy 1:7
SAVED: 24 years old
POSITIONS: Left Field and Second Base
2011 TEAM: Supervisor of Staff for Baseball Chapel
SCHOOL: California State University, Fullerton
DRAFTED: 16th Round of 1992 draft by Kansas City Royals
DEBUT: May 6, 2000 for Atlanta Braves
SEASONS: 2000 (Retired)
TEAMS: Braves and Orioles
NUMBER: 11

Humble yourselves before the Lord, and he will lift you up.
—James 4:10

We are called to be humble (1 Peter 5:5) and to keep our eyes on the prize. Jesus is the prize! Everything that we have, we have received as a blessing from the Lord. By being humble, we show our understanding that the Lord is the One in control. Being humble does not mean not working hard or not achieving through hard work. In fact, it means the opposite. Knowing that Jesus is the prize, each day we should work our hardest to glorify the Lord in all that we do. The past is the past, the future has yet to come, but right now we have the opportunity to serve the Lord.

Years	2000	H	5	SB	0
G	25	2B	0	CS	0
PA	30	3B	0	BB	3
AB	27	HR	1	SO	4
R	4	RBI	2	BA	.185

Humble

Steve Sisco

IT WAS FAITH DAY IN San Diego and a gentleman was hesitant to invite a friend to the event. But he attended and heard testimonies from several baseball players. On the car ride home he accepted Christ. Soon after, his life was cut short by a heart attack. When Steve Sisco, a former player with the Atlanta Braves, heard that story it made him realize how many times this gentleman had seen these players on the field while never knowing that Christ was the center of their lives. When he saw them talking passionately about their King, something resonated.

"Not only do I not take it for granted to share Christ with somebody, but to live a life of integrity in front of my teammates as well. I see them all the time, so it's really important to maintain (my) integrity."

Sisco's story of accepting Christ begins with his wife. In 1993, she went on a mission trip and received Christ. She told him about it, but he felt he wasn't going to let God stand in the way of their relationship. "Little did I know that God wasn't going to let me stand in between their relationship," he says. "I feel I was prayed into the Kingdom by my wife."

A snowmobile accident became Sisco's wake-up call. After breaking his back, neck and left arm, he felt the only thing he had in life was taken away. "All I knew was baseball," he says. But Sisco persevered and got back to the team halfway through the season in 1994, only to find that his position had been taken away. "I was sitting on a bench for the first time in my life. It's almost laughable to think back about the trials I was going through when you think of the persecution around the world."

While sitting on the bench, he met another player who was handling it well. He lived his life in a different way, and Sisco realized he wanted that as well. "This guy was living for others and not himself," he says. "That was a huge revelation for me."

In 1994 he finally said, "Where do I sign up?" Sisco began hanging out with the chapel leader and was given his first Bible. "From that point on, I realized that baseball was a platform and not a profession. I still pursued it and wanted it, but I didn't know how to go about living my life for Christ and for baseball."

It was a slow process for Sisco, but he finally relinquished baseball to God. In 1995 his wife said, "When you give baseball over to God, you'll get to the big leagues."

In 1999 he didn't make it to the big leagues, even though it was the best year of his career. "I didn't understand why God wasn't allowing it," he explains. "The next year I gave baseball to God. I said, 'I don't care where I am in baseball, out of baseball, in Double A, in Triple A, I just want to serve Jesus.' In 2000, at the age of 30, I had my first invite to Major League Spring Training with the Atlanta Braves." The following year he was traded to the Baltimore Orioles, and in 2002 Sisco retired from a league in Mexico.

But God had different plans for him.

"I wrote out a prayer and tears were falling on my keyboard," he says. "I wanted to talk about the Lord and felt God pulling me away from the game, but I was scared to give it up."

He took off his spikes and became a youth pastor. By the summer of 2002, Sisco was in full-time ministry. Three years later, he left the church to take a staff position with Baseball Chapel. "Looking back, I really do consider my career nothing, but God still uses it in my life to be able to connect with people," he says. "I feel a sense of belonging to a community, and I don't feel like that island anymore like when I played the game."

"God should be my treasure and my heart should be there. Everything I am doing should be for Him, not for self-righteousness."
—Landon Powell

Landon Powell

LANDON REED POWELL

BORN: March 19, 1982 in Raleigh, NC
FAVORITE BIBLE VERSES: Colossians 3:23 and Matthew 6:21
SAVED: 12 years old
POSITIONS: Catcher and First Base
2011 TEAM: Oakland Athletics
SCHOOL: University of South Carolina
DRAFTED: 1st Round of 2004 draft by Oakland Athletics
DEBUT: April 11, 2009 for Oakland Athletics
SEASONS: 2009 – 2011 (Active)
TEAMS: Athletics
NUMBER: 35, 11
ACCOMPLISHMENTS: Caught Perfect Game: May 9, 2010

For where your treasure is, there your heart will be also.
—Matthew 6:21

Have you ever dreamed of being Indiana Jones running through a tunnel and finding a great treasure made of gold and diamonds? Indiana always ended up in a situation where he had to decide between his gold treasure and helping others. He always chose to give up on his dream treasure and save the people in need. His true treasure was not made of gold and diamonds.

We are called to set our hearts on Jesus as our treasure—not money and possessions. When we do this, our lives will change. We should strive to glorify the Lord in everything that we do. Our place in heaven with Jesus is the biggest treasure we could ever imagine.

Years	2009-2011	H	75	SB	1
G	123	2B	14	CS	0
PA	406	3B	0	BB	40
AB	363	HR	10	SO	97
R	42	RBI	45	BA	.207

Treasure

Landon Powell

LANDON POWELL HAS A SPECIAL pair of shoes for the ballfield. What makes them unique? He can look down and see the Bible verse Colossians 3:23, "Whatever you do, work at it with all your heart, as working for the Lord, not for men," which he wrote on his shoes as a reminder that he's playing for the Lord.

"My whole life I was playing baseball and I made baseball my treasure," he said. "God should be my treasure and my heart should be there also. Everything I'm doing should be for Him."

For twenty years Powell focused on the game of baseball. He finally realized that it was just another job and the big leagues weren't everything he imagined they would be. Christ's love was the only thing that could fulfill him. "Throughout some injuries, I realized I was doing things for the wrong reasons. I was doing it for me and not for Him."

Being a Christian baseball player was challenging at times, especially in the clubhouse, he said. "There are 25 of us together and 20 of them probably aren't Christians. People are always cussing. It's hard to make sure you're praying." If you're a Christian, you are held to a higher standard, he pointed out. "You get called out quicker. It's a very tough game and full of heartbreak, disappointment and failure. So it's difficult when you fail that much and deal with all that adversity. It is very difficult to stay on a path with God."

An encounter with another Christian helped him. While playing in Los Angeles, he met the owner of the Christian clothing line Not of This World. He heard the man's testimony, and it fired him up spiritually. Last season there were more Christians on the team, more Bible studies, and they attended chapel on Sundays. "I definitely think God was working," he said.

Powell tried his best to separate himself from the live and die by the game of baseball where your mood depends on how well you play that day. Powell now knows his life is about what God put him on earth to do. He's using his experiences to glorify the Lord and talk about Him to others. Powell was diagnosed with a liver disease that he will have for the rest of his life. But he kept playing and his disease has improved. "God has been there," he said. Because of his illness, Powell has become involved with two organizations: Donate Life South Carolina and Donors on the Diamond.

"I now make it a point to make God the main focus of my talks," he said. "I let people know that I wouldn't be able to do anything if it wasn't for Him." His life began to change even more his first year in the big leagues from 2008 to 2009. Powell and his wife got involved with Professional Athlete Outreach.

Powell believes sports are just another way to spread God's word. "If people in sports could use the game, baseball or football or whatever, as a platform to speak and talk about God, if that brings one more person closer to Christ, then that's what God wanted."

"There are always trials and tribulations throughout your life that you look back on or face today. I can remember lying down in my bed every night saying my prayers in college and having that personal time that gives you peace to lie down and sleep soundly."
—Britt Reames

Britt Reames

WILLIAM BRITT REAMES

BORN: August 19, 1973 in Seneca, SC
FAVORITE BIBLE VERSES: Philippians 4:6 and the Book of John
SAVED: Teenager
POSITIONS: Pitcher
2011 TEAM: Assistant Baseball Coach at Furman University
SCHOOL: The Citadel
DRAFTED: 17th Round of 1995 draft by St. Louis Cardinals
DEBUT: August 20, 2000 for St. Louis Cardinals
SEASONS: 2000 – 2006 (Retired)
TEAMS: Cardinals, Expos, Athletics, and Pirates
NUMBERS: 68, 34, 57, 56

Therefore, my brothers, you whom I love and long for, my joy and crown, that is how you should stand firm in the Lord, dear friends!
—Philippians 4:1

Jesus is the firm rock that our foundation should be built upon. He will not waver in times of distress or temptation, and He will always be there for us. The Lord has given us a direct link to communicate with him—prayer. It is our responsibility to spend personal time with the Lord in prayer and in the Word. Through this personal time, He will build us a firm foundation.

He lifted me out of the slimy pit, out of the mud and mire; he set my feet on a rock and gave me a firm place to stand.
—Psalm 40:2

Years	2000-2006	L	13		ER	128
G	101	SV	0		HR	32
GS	26	IP	218.0		BB	118
ERA	5.28	H	226		SO	204
W	7	R	145			

Firm

Britt Reames

AS A BASEBALL COACH FOR Furman University, Britt Reames makes sure he remains strong in his walk with Christ. "I try to lead by example and show them how happy, humble and patient I am," he said. "God has given me those traits to handle the students and talk to them the right way."

"It's not only about winning but (about) developing young men," Reames said. "We have great Christians on the team. There are times we talk about our faith on the field and where they are in their walk and what they are doing to love Jesus."

Reames was exposed to Christianity early in his life. He grew up in a Baptist church and accepted Christ as a teenager. "When I was between 13 and 15 years old, I really started to understand that you have to live your life with faith and have a personal relationship with Him."

When he joined the Minor Leagues and eventually the St. Louis Cardinals, it wasn't too hard a transition as far as his faith went. "I was fortunate because each team always had a group of guys that were believers. We would have a time of fellowship every Sunday."

Having faith in Jesus helped Reames to remain a strong ball-player. "I was given my abilities through Him. I'm playing for Him. It's not just for yourself or teammates."

While at spring training, his faith in Christ was tested when his fiancée was killed in a car accident. "There is no way I would have gotten through that situation unless I was a strong believer." Getting through it meant he was in the Word every night and talking to the chaplains. "The Lord gave me peace about what happened. I knew I only had one place to go and that was to Him."

"To this day I'm probably not as good of a Christian as I was then," he said. "At that point I was locked in with His armor. You ask yourself 'How can I get back to that?' With having a wife and kids, you have to slow down and arm yourself."

Reames and his wife were recently blessed with a son. Having a child has helped their marriage become even stronger, Reames said. "Reading the baby Bible and looking at cartoon books about Jesus has helped us in our walk as a couple."

He knows that consistency is important: "There are so many times that you don't do anything (such as read the Bible) for a few days and you lose it. You have to stay in it and surround yourself with other Christians. You need to sit together and pray together. When your heart isn't fully with Jesus, there is a void in there. It's a matter of what are you going to do about it?"

"The biggest blessing we can ever have is to know Jesus and to know this life is not for us even though we are here. We are here for God's glory. I am thankful He chose me and I know my sins are forgiven."
—Stephen Drew

Stephen Drew

STEPHEN ORIS DREW

BORN: March 16, 1983 in Hahira, GA

FAVORITE BIBLE VERSES: John 4:1-9 and Titus 3:5

SAVED: 10 years old

POSITIONS: Shortstop

2011 TEAM: Arizona Diamondbacks

SCHOOL: Florida State University

DRAFTED: 1st Round of 2004 draft by Arizona Diamondbacks

DEBUT: July 15, 2006 for Arizona Diamondbacks

SEASONS: 2006 – 2011 (Active)

TEAMS: Diamondbacks

NUMBER: 6

He saved us, not because of righteous things we had done, but because of his mercy. He saved us through the washing of rebirth and renewal by the Holy Spirit.
—Titus 3:5

For a Christian, the most comfortable feeling we have is the assurance that we are saved. Saved from our sins. Even on our best days, we still fall short of perfection. Whether by accident or by decisions we make, we do something wrong every day. We are forgiven through Jesus because He stepped up for us—coming to earth for us, living a perfect life, and dying the death each of us deserved. No wonder we call Him Savior.

Who has saved us and called us to a holy life—not because of anything we have done but because of his own purpose and grace.
—2 Timothy 1:9

Years	2006-2011	H	750	SB	33
G	733	2B	168	CS	13
PA	3090	3B	51	BB	256
AB	2782	HR	70	SO	528
R	376	RBI	321	BA	.270

Saved

Stephen Drew

STEPHEN DREW'S BIGGEST BLESSING IS quite simple…knowing Jesus as his Lord and Savior. "This life is not for us," he said. "We're here for God's glory. I'm so thankful He chose me and I know my sins are forgiven."

As a Christian, Drew said that every day is a work in progress for him and his faith. "We're not perfect as Christians, but I'm trying to become more like Him," Drew said. "He has grace on me and saved me from eternal damnation."

Prior to graduating from high school, Drew didn't know if he was ready to go out and play pro baseball. He saw his two older brothers Tim and J.D. go two different routes and how successful they both were in the sport. He decided to attend college, but he had to take a difficult test in order to go to college. "I knew it was up to the Lord and wherever He wants me I was supposed to go," Drew said. "I remember sitting there and feeling peace and comfort that I haven't felt before."

He passed the test but still wasn't sure what the best decision would be—attending college or going to the minors. "Here it is. It's yours," he said to God. "I trust that your plan is better than mine."

"As humans, we think our plan is best when it's really kind of opposite," Drew said. "The Lord knows best." Drew attended Florida State University where he played college ball. The Arizona Diamondbacks drafted him in the first round in 2004.

In 2007 Drew had a frustrating season. "I thought I had a really good season hitting-wise. However, I wasn't getting many hits and couldn't understand it because I was hitting balls hard," he said. The season was both a test of character for him and a test to see where he was spiritually as a Christian.

"There are tough times where you get mad at the game," Drew said. "(You ask) how am I helping the team, what am I telling guys and how am I acting? People watch your actions. Especially when you say you are a Christian and follower of Jesus Christ."

"Sometimes when times get tough, you may not think He's there," he said. "It's an amazing feeling to watch Him at work in everyday life." Drew has had a chance to share the good news of the Lord with teammates through tough times. "You are frustrated from the season but blessed. You have guys who come up and say, 'What is it? You had a down year, but you are still the same person and act the same toward all the guys. How do you do it?' Then you can share Christ with them."

When times do get tough and he's away from his family travelling, Drew knows the Lord is there every step of the way. "One of the verses that sticks with me is Joshua 1:9: "Have I not commanded you? Be strong and courageous. Do not be terrified; do not be discouraged, for the LORD your God will be with you wherever you go."

Another thing that helps Drew on the road is being a part of Baseball Chapel, a ministry that serves those in professional baseball who desire to deepen their Christian faith but who are unable to attend church. "I am thankful to have that time with the Lord through our profession," he said.

As a Christian, Drew knows he needs to always be obedient and stay focused on what we're really here for. "We love to play the game, but as Christians it's not who we are. It's not what defines us," he stressed. "We understand Jesus is sovereign. We're here for a reason and that's to glorify His name."

"It was quite a journey. We became Christians and it was very freeing. I felt like I was carrying the world and my life on my shoulders...to turn that over to the Lord and have a guidance and anchor now for the first time. God gave me an amazing gift to pitch, to play baseball, and to handle pressure. I got to the Major Leagues, and it helped to handle the pressure when I knew the Lord was in control. He gave me the ability, and it was my obligation to do the very best I could with it and then to turn it over to Him the best I could."
—Tim Burke

Tim Burke

TIMOTHY PHILIP BURKE

BORN: February 19, 1959 in Omaha, NE

FAVORITE BIBLE VERSES: Jeremiah 29:11, 1 Peter 5:7, and Matthew 11:20-30

SAVED: August 25, 1982

POSITIONS: Pitcher

2011 TEAM: Hockey Ministries International

SCHOOL: University of Nebraska

DRAFTED: 2nd Round of 1980 draft by Pittsburgh Pirates

DEBUT: April 8, 1985 for Montreal Expos

SEASONS: 1985 – 1992 (Retired)

TEAMS: Expos, Mets, and Yankees

NUMBERS: 54, 44, 41

ACCOMPLISHMENTS: All Star Selection—1989; Author of—*Major League Dad—The Moving Story of an All-Star Pitcher Who Gave up Baseball for His Family*

"For I know the plans I have for you," declares the Lord, "plans to prosper you and not to harm you, plans to give you hope and a future."
—Jeremiah 29:11

Surrendering our lives to Christ is one of the hardest things for us to do. We want to be in control of our lives. The truth is that we are not in control. It was by the grace of God that He saved us from our sins. The Lord showed us mercy because He loves us. The Lord has a plan for each of us, and it is our responsibility to surrender our lives completely over to Him. This means our time and our money, being obedient to the Lord, serving in the community, and being in the Word every day.

Years	1985-1992	L	33	ER	211
G	498	SV	102	HR	49
GS	2	IP	699.1	BB	219
ERA	2.72	H	624	SO	444
W	49	R	251		

Grace

Tim Burke

TIM BURKE CAN TELL YOU firsthand that even if you become a Christian it doesn't mean you won't go through heartache and pain. He is actually grateful for the difficulties in his life because it has brought him closer to the Lord.

Burke's personal struggles had nothing to do with baseball but concerned his family. He and his wife adopted five children from different countries. All of them have special needs. One young girl was from Korea and had heart problems that required surgery. There were complications with the heart surgery, and now she is mentally handicapped. "It still is difficult," said Burke. "But she has taught us more about the Lord than anything we've ever experienced. She's amazing and the most unconditionally loving person."

It also put a bit of strain on his marriage. "We felt the Lord took care of us for a lot of years and now all of a sudden He fell off the radar screen. I got really mad at Him," he said. "I turned my back on Him and said, 'To heck with Him if He's forgotten about me.'"

But the Lord didn't give up on Burke. "In the midst of all that and my disobedience, He did some things that only He could do. You could almost see Him sneaking around the corner. He would do the most amazing things leaving fingerprints all over our lives and our journeys." Burke said he realized God was still there during some dark days. "I started learning more about grace and saw my sin a lot more. I saw how much He loved me in the midst of that and that drew me closer to Him."

In the 1980s Burke had been at the top of his game with his total focus on baseball. He was pitching badly and began drinking to try to cope. He was married in 1982, but Christine was soon ready to get a divorce due to his bad lifestyle choices. Then things began to change when he was "talked into" attending a Bible study. "Life was kind of crappy, so I figured it wouldn't make it any worse," he said. He and his wife left the Bible study intrigued by the good news of Jesus.

"(My wife) kept giving me extensions on our marriage. I started reading the Bible and began seeing my sin more and more." By the end of his difficult baseball season he ran across the Bible verse in 1 Peter 5:7 which says, "Cast all your anxiety on him because he cares for you."

"I realized Jesus cares about me so much that He wants me to give Him my problems and worries and cares," Burke said. "It started to click that this is about a whole love relationship."

On August 25, 1982 he and his wife gave their lives to Christ. "Both of us couldn't run from the Lord any longer. It was an enormous blessing, and we are still married 28 years later. Looking back, the Lord put us together for a reason. It was really a blessing that we came to the Lord together."

When Burke made his way to the Major Leagues in 1985, knowing Christ helped him to navigate through temptations and the intoxication of success, money and fame. "That was huge for me," he said.

Tim and Christine Burke are well known for being Christians and holding Bible studies. They also work with Hockey Ministries International to help minister to hockey players and their families at all levels of the game.

"Me—and everyone else on earth—we are just prone to think about ourselves more than Him," he said. "It's a big journey that we're on and, hopefully, a few years from now I will be further along than I am now. It's made me hunger for Him more."

"God is the one who made me, and He gifted me to play the game of baseball. I believe that He gifts an individual for His glory and not for our own whatsoever. The reason I played professional baseball was to do what I am doing now. It wasn't just for me, it was for His glory."
—Bryan Hickerson

Bryan Hickerson

BRYAN DAVID HICKERSON

BORN: October 13, 1963 in Bemidji, MN
FAVORITE BIBLE VERSES: Philippians 1
SAVED: 11 years old
POSITIONS: Pitcher
2011 TEAM: Operations Director/Military for Unlimited Potential Inc.
SCHOOL: University of Minnesota
DRAFTED: 7th Round of 1986 draft by Minnesota Twins
DEBUT: July 25, 1991 for San Francisco Giants
SEASONS: 1991-1995 (Retired)
TEAMS: Giants, Cubs, and Rockies
NUMBERS: 41, 47

For to me, to live is Christ and to die is gain.
—Philippians 1:21

The Lord has blessed each of us with talents and gifts. Whether these gifts are in baseball, writing, teaching, or other skills, they were given to us to glorify Jesus. It is our responsibility to recognize the talents we have and to use them to serve Him by serving others.

Each one should use whatever gift he has received to serve others, faithfully administering God's grace in its various forms.
—1 Peter 4:10

Years	1991-1995	L	21		ER	212	
G	209	SV	2		HR	52	
GS	36	IP	404.1		BB	143	
ERA	4.72	H	451		SO	279	
W	21	R	221				

Gifted

Bryan Hickerson

BRYAN HICKERSON IS DOING SOMETHING he never thought he would do—working full time in ministry with Unlimited Potential Inc. Traveling the world is allowing him the opportunity to share his faith with others from Germany and Italy to Thailand and Africa. He has also been ministering to our military men and women in Iraq and Afghanistan.

"I never imagined this or dreamed it," he said. "While I was playing pro ball I would have laughed at them if someone told me I'd be doing this after my playing days were over. But the Lord radically changed my view of things."

Discipleship is one of the core values of UPI, and its mission is to share the great news of God through the game of baseball. Evangelistic camps and clinics have taken place in the United States and around the world. Since 1997, UPI has teamed up with the US military by ministering to service members worldwide.

"Early on, these mission trips impacted me in a different way and now it's an even deeper level," Hickerson said. "This is what faith is about. It's a global thing and it opened my eyes to that. Now it's refined growth as to what God is going to show me on a trip. It's amazing to me every time."

Often when he's speaking to a group, Hickerson can't help but share an amusing story with others. It was the seventh inning and he was on the mound pitching at Candlestick Park his last year in the big leagues. (He played for the Giants for many years and then the Chicago Cubs.) His habit was to jog back to the dugout with eyes on the ground, so as not to be distracted by the surroundings. He began jogging back to the dugout, looking down as he always did. But he was heading the wrong way.

"I heard a voice say, 'Hey Hick. Where are you going?'" I was at the chalk line and noticed my jersey said Cubs. I was headed to the wrong dugout, to my old team, the Giants. I use that story sometimes when I speak." He then asks, "Where are you going?" "Who are you really?" and "Are you wearing your own righteousness (old team) or the righteousness of God (His gift)?" These thoughts also help him reflect on how far he's come in his relationship with Christ.

As a child, Hickerson was competitive when it came to memorizing verses from the Bible. "God was using His Word to draw me in and make Himself known. The reality of the truth of the passages hit me, and I believed."

Those beliefs began to take hold of Hickerson during his first year in the Minor Leagues. He began to have a true desire to walk with God. "God knows for sure when I was truly converted. I knew He was going to use me for something."

And his faith in God has been tested.

Hickerson sat out for a year after having "Tommy John" surgery (reconstruction of the elbow). "God tested my faith to see if He was my treasure or not." He found that having that opportunity was invaluable. "I said, 'This is one of God's greatest gifts to me.' It allowed me to evaluate whether He was my treasure or getting to the big leagues was my treasure."

When he decided to go into the ministry full time, he asked a pastor what was the most valuable thing in ministry. The answer was that the hardest things people have to do are the most important things. "The only reason I live and breathe should be to glorify Him," said Hickerson. "To really own that is a challenge for every believer. If you live that, there wouldn't be an anemic community of believers. We would be powerful witnesses."

He says the "wow" factor that comes into play when first believing the Gospel should never go away. "Keep finding that treasure and continue to bask in it. Looking back, I believe God made me to play baseball. I entirely believe now that the reason I played professional ball is to do what I'm doing now. It wasn't for me at all, at least in the way the world sees it. It was for His glory."

We know also that the Son of God has come and has given us understanding, so that we may know him who is true. And we are in him who is true by being in his Son Jesus Christ. He is the true God and eternal life.

1 John 5:20

"This is the one piece of God's Word that made the most sense to me, trust in Him. I am a finite man and God is infinite, lean on Him and not my own understanding."
—Tim Salmon

Tim Salmon

TIMOTHY JAMES SALMON

BORN: August 24, 1968 in Long Beach, CA

FAVORITE BIBLE VERSES: Proverbs 3:5-6

SAVED: College

POSITIONS: Right Field

2011 TEAM: Tim Salmon Foundation

SCHOOL: Grand Canyon University

DRAFTED: 3rd Round of 1989 draft by California Angels

DEBUT: August 21, 1992 for California Angels

SEASONS: 1992 – 2006 (Retired)

TEAMS: Angels

NUMBER: 15

ACCOMPLISHMENTS: American League Rookie of the Year—1993; Silver Slugger Award—1995; Hutch Award—2002; World Series Champions—2002; Founder of the Tim Salmon Foundation; Author of—*Always an Angel: Playing the Game with Fire and Faith*

Trust in the Lord with all your heart and lean not on your own understanding; in all your ways acknowledge him, and he will make your paths straight.
—Proverbs 3:5-6

When we have an understanding that the Lord is all powerful, then we know that we need to trust Him each and every day. This understanding allows us to lay our worries in the Lord's hands. In return, we can focus everything that we do into glorifying Jesus.

Years	1992-2006	H	1674	SB	48
G	1672	2B	339	CS	42
PA	7039	3B	24	BB	970
AB	5934	HR	299	SO	1360
R	986	RBI	1016	BA	.282

Understanding

Tim Salmon

WHEN TIM SALMON PLAYED HIS last game with the Angels, something unexpected happened—God used the opportunity to teach His grace and mercy one last time. Salmon didn't quite shine in his final at bat, popping up a ball to the shortstop with the game on the line. The Angels ended up losing the game, but the crowd gave Salmon one final standing ovation.

"Here I am walking back to the dugout in disgust and the crowd (is) saying "we still love you," Salmon said. "It struck me. Isn't this what God is saying to us every day? The fans looked beyond my mistake and wanted to show me their appreciation. You fall on your face, but God says, 'Hey. Stand up and come before me. My grace, mercy, and love is abundant.'"

"That moment encapsulated my entire professional career," he said. "That was a very powerful moment in my life."

Salmon was raised Catholic, but he wouldn't say he was a Christian. He believed in God and heaven, but there was no evidence of a relationship with Jesus in his life. In high school someone introduced him to the idea of Christianity, but he wasn't very interested at the time. He then received a scholarship to a small Southern Baptist school, Grand Canyon College. He was surprised to see both chapel and Old Testament history on his class schedule.

"I didn't realize it was a Baptist college," he said with a chuckle. "I was just going for baseball and a business degree." He befriended a Christian teammate and began asking questions about Jesus. "My friend helped me make sense of everything I was hearing in the classroom." One night over dinner with a friend, he accepted Christ as his Lord and Savior. "I remember praying for a new direction in my life."

After accepting the Lord, Salmon began praying that the Lord would bring new friends into his life to help him build on his faith, and the Lord did just that. He found a few Christians that became close friends, and they began a discipleship group. Reading his Bible daily, his faith began to grow stronger.

While he was learning about the Bible, two verses really made an impact on Salmon: "Trust in the Lord with all your heart and lean not on your own understanding; in all your ways acknowledge Him, and He will make your paths straight." (Proverbs 3:5-6)

"It encapsulated the essence of what Christ was all about," he said. "That was my heart's verse. This is one piece of God's word that makes the most sense to me when I am going through trials. Trust in Him. Lean on Him and not my own understanding. That verse covers everything. It's a simple verse about the kind of faith we are to exhibit during trials, and it brings about hope."

"I knew I needed direction, and knew I was being influenced by the wrong things," he said. "My perspective changed and everything seemed to fall into place. I had a Heavenly Father that I could trust and rely on through the good and bad. The most comfort came in knowing that He is in control and there is a plan."

Sometimes that plan didn't make sense, such as when he was dealing with major injuries during his baseball career. "Those are times where you hang onto the Word of God and know that it's an opportunity to practice and develop your faith. You learn that our walk is a daily journey, and God has an ultimate design for us."

Salmon is glad he became a Christian before making his way to the Major Leagues. It helped him to avoid getting caught up in a world of fame and fortune. "God is at work behind me," he said. "It's for His glory and not mine."

He knows that he has been abundantly blessed with a wife, four children and a foundation that allows him to help others. The Tim Salmon Foundation supports charities assisting abused and at-risk children as well as faith-based organizations, he explained. "We reach out to kids through foundations and serve as a mentor and role model. We make a difference in people's lives. There are so many opportunities to do things because of my success on the ball field."

And the God of all grace, who called you to his eternal glory in Christ, after you have suffered a little while, will himself restore you and make you strong, firm and steadfast.

1 Peter 5:10

"Nothing is as important as serving God daily. When He puts something on your heart, you may want to say no but you'd better get to yes in a hurry."
—Steve Foster

Steve Foster

STEVEN EUGENE FOSTER

BORN: August 16, 1966 in Dallas, TX

FAVORITE BIBLE VERSES: Romans 1:16

SAVED: 8 years old

POSITIONS: Pitcher

2011 TEAM: Pitching Coach for the Kansas City Royals

SCHOOL: University of Texas at Arlington

DRAFTED: 12th Round of 1988 draft by Cincinnati Reds

DEBUT: August 22, 1991 for Cincinnati Reds

SEASONS: 1991 – 1993 (Retired)

TEAMS: Reds

NUMBER: 54

ACCOMPLISHMENTS: Co-Author of—*Lessons from Little League and Life*

I am not ashamed of the gospel, because it is the power of God for the salvation of everyone who believes: first for the Jew, then for the Gentile.
—Romans 1:16

As followers of Christ, the Lord has a plan for us. At times the Holy Spirit inside us will give a direction, a feeling, or even a sense of heaviness prompting us to do something for the Lord. We will be called. It is our responsibility to listen and respond to our callings. When we respond, the Lord will bless others or us in ways we can never imagine.

Years	1991-1993	L	3	ER	24
G	59	SV	2	HR	6
GS	1	IP	89.2	BB	22
ERA	2.41	H	82	SO	61
W	3	R	29		

Called

Steve Foster

MANY TIMES THE LORD HAS a different plan in mind, and Steve Foster knew he had to be open to it during a 2004 mission trip to the Dominican Republic. It was supposed to be a simple trip in which he and several high school students would lead Vacation Bible School and work with students 25 miles east of Haiti. Once they arrived, they learned that they would be helping victims of a devastating flood.

Not only did the trip have an impact on the students and Foster, but they helped change the lives of individuals. One such person was a Haitian woman who came down a mountain with a newborn baby in need of help. She unknowingly crossed into the Dominican Republic—a definite no-no in that area. Missionaries saw her, picked her up and brought her back to the clinic. After her baby underwent several surgeries for a cleft palate, Foster, a youth pastor, and several others had to get her back home, which was not an easy feat and was dangerous.

"All of us were crying and thinking this was the ultimate sacrifice," said Foster. "We've had moments in our lives that were life-changing but pulling out of the clinic that day and not knowing where we were going, we were willing to sacrifice our lives to get this woman back home with her baby and to help these people."

Foster and his group had to travel through four or five guard stations, manned by young men with machine guns who were willing to take their lives, as they tried to get the woman back home. "As we got through each one, our boldness and self sacrifice became stronger."

As they dropped her off with rice and beans for her family, the group was trusting God to get them back safely. On the way back, something unexpected happened that gave them an opportunity to serve Christ and share His love with others. As they were led to a home on the side of a hill, a woman covered in warts greeted them and was in need of prayer.

"My first thought was to protect myself, but at that moment it became a time to serve Christ for this woman. She was crying crocodile tears. We all loved on her and left food with them. We were crying and singing praises."

When they returned, they were thanking God for the unbelievable and incredible day He gave them. Through the next week, Foster preached from Matthew 5 to the youth. He saw lives being changed as he visited many baseball fields and spoke to young Dominican Republic baseball players.

"God spoke to my heart, 'You were willing to give it all. I will take you back into baseball and you will serve me.' It was clear God wanted me on that trip and for His reasons."

Foster found his way back into the game of baseball and began coaching in the big leagues, although it wasn't something he really wanted to do because of the sacrifices it calls for. "I'm gone from my family and justifying it comes only at the foot of the cross for me and my family," he said. "It comes at a price, and the price is my service to the Lord. And there is no greater joy in my life."

He is now teaching ball players the Word of God and building meaningful relationships with others. "I'm praying that He would bring people into my life because that's the core of why He put us on the planet. Life relationships are where change takes place… not in teaching a curve ball. I know what I'm called to do. The Lord put on my heart many years ago to serve Him fully."

God's plan wasn't always clear to Foster. After accepting Christ at the age of eight, two years later Foster had to deal with the divorce of his parents. It threw a curve ball into his trust of others and of the Lord. He began to fall away from Christ, but his relationship with Him was ignited once again when he began attending church regularly. "I was able to see God's plan for my life through all of those stages," he said. "It's about our shortcomings and it's only through Christ that we're even where we are this very day."

He is enjoying every minute of where his life has led him. Working with the young ball players God has brought into his life and hearing life-change stories warms his heart. "Changed lives change lives," he said. "I can see what He's doing. I'm simply here to share the story with anybody that will listen."

"I can say I'm truly an ambassador for Christ in the game of baseball."

If any of you lacks wisdom, you should ask God, who gives generously to all without finding fault, and it will be given to you. But when you ask, you must believe and not doubt, because the one who doubts is like a wave of the sea, blown and tossed by the wind.

James 1:5-6

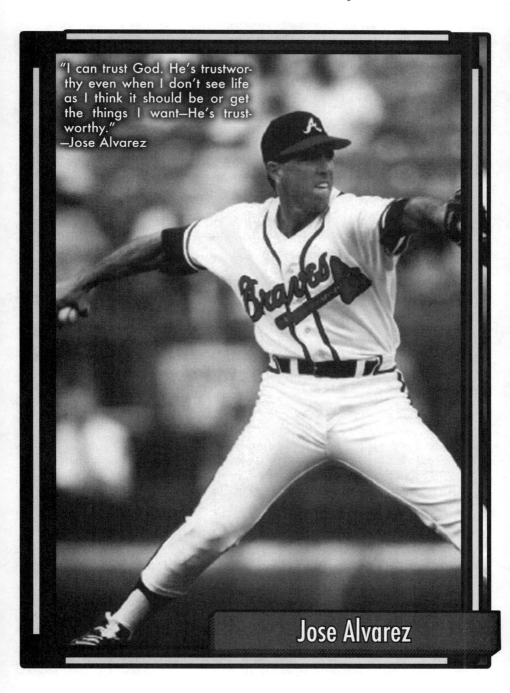

"I can trust God. He's trustworthy even when I don't see life as I think it should be or get the things I want—He's trustworthy."
—Jose Alvarez

Jose Alvarez

JOSE LINO ALVAREZ

BORN: April 12, 1956 in Tampa, FL

FAVORITE BIBLE VERSES: John 14:6, Proverbs 3:5-6, and Philippians 4:6-9

SAVED: College

POSITIONS: Pitcher

2011 TEAM: FCA Nationwide TOURLIFE Golf Representative

SCHOOL: University of Louisiana at Lafayette

DRAFTED: 8th Round of 1978 draft by Atlanta Braves

DEBUT: October 1, 1981 for Atlanta Braves

SEASONS: 1981 – 1989, (1990 on disabled list) (Retired)

TEAMS: Braves and Giants

NUMBERS: 50, 40, 41

Finally, brothers, whatever is true, whatever is noble, whatever is right, whatever is pure, whatever is lovely, whatever is admirable-if anything is excellent or praiseworthy-think about such things. Whatever you have learned or received or heard from me, or seen in me-put it into practice. And the God of peace will be with you.
—Philippians 4:8-9

The Lord gave Solomon an opportunity to ask for whatever he wanted. Solomon asked for wisdom. Wisdom is a more valuable treasure than any amount of gold or silver. With wisdom we can understand what the Lord desires in our lives and what His plans are for us. With wisdom we are able to serve the Lord with all of our heart.

Years	1981-1989	L	9	ER	54
G	98	SV	5	HR	12
GS	0	IP	162.1	BB	79
ERA	2.99	H	140	SO	134
W	8	R	56		

Wisdom

Jose Alvarez

JOSE ALVAREZ IS A GLASS half-full kind of guy. And his trust in God keeps that glass from becoming empty.

"I may not be the smartest guy around, but I usually don't have to hit my head against the wall too many times to realize it hurts. The best lesson is I can trust God and He's trustworthy even when I don't see life as I think it should be or get the things I want," he said. "Essentially what we're called to do is trust. When you trust, you will obey and come to grow and love that person."

But that trust in God wasn't always there. While in college, he basically had no direction but knew he wanted to play baseball. "I was living in the world my way thinking there was a God but living as though I thought *I* was God." His senior year he almost lost his opportunity to play ball when he was placed on academic and disciplinary probation. That was a wake-up call for Alvarez, but attending a meeting changed his life.

He was invited to a Fellowship of Christian Athletes (FCA) meeting on campus. He realized God was saying, "Dude. You got some issues that you need to look at. Look to Me to be your answer and stop looking and chasing the world." It was there that he learned of God's grace. A week later he accepted Christ as his Lord and Savior. "I realized it wasn't about me inviting God into my life, but about accepting the call from God and His invitation to invite me into His story."

After his senior year the Atlanta Braves drafted Alvarez. Two years later while at spring training he suffered an injury. That ended up being another wake up-call for him. "God was saying, 'Get off the middle of the road. Serve Me, love Me or hate Me.' I was in a place in my life where I was looking back at the things that I thought would fulfill me rather than enjoying and growing in the relationship with God. I wasn't surrendering. And while I knew Jesus, at times my life was lived as though it was all about me."

As his faith grew, he was excited about sharing it with others, especially his new teammates. After tearing his pitching elbow ligament during spring training with the San Francisco Giants, he began to see and experience some challenges of being a Christian. "Some guys were harsh in their remarks and critical of my faith. I didn't lose sleep over it, but the boiling point was when I came back from my injury." A few players with star status were vocal about their dislike for Christians. Alvarez recalls a player's words: "If we could just get rid of a few more Christians on this team, we'll be okay."

The Giants released him, in their words, due to his off-the-field activities and influence with other players. "I knew it had nothing to do with my progress and rehab from the injury, but (was) because of my faith. I was attending Christian camps, sharing my testimony and when the players would ask about my faith I would share it. I called MLB to file a grievance but they wouldn't hear my case."

Did Alvarez see it as persecution? He knew that God was using it for a reason. "It was something God used to show me He is in control. I learned a valuable lesson—one that I continue to learn—I can trust God."

"Where I am right now is exactly where God wants me," he said. "It's about Him not about me."

"If I didn't feel like this is where God has me for a reason, I would have moved on by now. I enjoy playing baseball and my dream in life is playing Major League Baseball. God has kept me in the game for a reason."
—Gabe Gross

Gabe Gross

GABRIEL JORDAN GROSS

BORN: October 21, 1979 in Baltimore, MD
FAVORITE BIBLE VERSES: Proverbs 3:5-6 and Romans 12:1
SAVED: 9 years old
POSITIONS: Outfield
SCHOOL: Auburn University
DRAFTED: 1st Round of 2001 draft by Toronto Blue Jays
DEBUT: August 7, 2004 for Toronto Blue Jays
SEASONS: 2004 – 2010 (Retired)
TEAMS: Blue Jays, Rays, Brewers, and Athletics
NUMBERS: 21, 18, 14, 26

Therefore, I urge you, brothers, in view of God's mercy, to offer your bodies as living sacrifices, holy and pleasing to God—this is your spiritual act of worship.
—Romans 12:1

The Lord has the right to destroy us; after all, He created us. However, He chose to show us mercy. Jesus chose to die on the cross to save us from our sins. If we allow the Lord to have control of our lives, He will place us where He wants us for a reason. This includes in every area of our lives: family, work, school...everything. Jesus asks that we surrender our bodies to Him each and every day so that He can be in control. Part of our surrender is that we are to show mercy and forgiveness to those who do us wrong.

Years	2004-2010	H	349	SB	22
G	657	2B	78	CS	10
PA	1680	3B	8	BB	199
AB	1461	HR	40	SO	349
R	203	RBI	186	BA	.239

Mercy

Gabe Gross

GABE GROSS' BIGGEST DECISION IN his life was to follow Christ, and his hardest decision was to stop playing football. Gross played both football and baseball at Auburn. During his sophomore year, he felt a need to concentrate on one or the other. "I loved playing football and loved baseball too. My dad played football for Auburn. All my life I wanted to go to Auburn and play football." He spent a lot of time praying about it and realized that God had a plan all along.

Right after Gross played his first baseball game his freshman year at Auburn, he signed a baseball to give to the athletic director, but he lost the ball. "I could not find it anywhere. I looked in my apartment and the ball was not there. I turned everything over."

Nearly a year later, while trying to make the decision on which sport to play he was on the floor praying. "I got through praying and with my head on the floor I opened my eyes and was looking underneath my bed. The baseball was sitting right there. I knew in my heart what to do," he said. "It was tough because I loved football, but God led me to baseball. It was a smart decision in my life. It has led to a lot of opportunities to explain His name."

Gross was able to share the good news of Christ with other ballplayers and knows he played the game for a reason. Playing baseball helped Gross see how much he needed Christ in his life. "I realized how much I needed Him when I was forced to put up with what happens in Major League Baseball." There were plenty of times when he was the only one on the team trying to follow Christ. And the opposite was true: times when he could fellowship with several Christian teammates.

"The help that having other brothers in Christ with you is immeasurable in the game of baseball," he said. Some days he and his teammates would spend time in the Bible for several hours after a game. One of Gross' favorite Bible verses is Proverbs 3:5-6. "Trust in the LORD with all your heart and lean not on your own understanding; in all your ways submit to him, and he will make your paths straight."

"If you take it word by word and implement what it says, it takes on a whole new meaning," he said. "It's one thing to say it's a great verse and another to base your life on it. Understand that God is a whole lot bigger than you are. You just have to follow Him and trust that what's best for His Kingdom is what you're going to do."

There were times when it was difficult for Gross to see the bigger picture. He and his wife suffered miscarriages before being able to have a child. He was on the road and wasn't able to be there for his wife during some of that time.

"I spent a lot of time in prayer, and a year later we had our first baby," he said. "I know all things work together for His good. I know He'll take care of us. Those are a lot of things that I relied on to try and get me through." He realizes it's not always roses and rainbows when you're a Christian. "There are a lot of warnings Christ gives about suffering and discomfort when you dedicate your life to Him," he said.

Gross accepted Jesus as his Lord and Savior at the age of nine. He talked to his mom about it every night for a couple of weeks. "She did the best she could to answer, and it got to be real to me. I gave my life to Him. I don't want to think about where I would be if what Jesus taught in Scripture wasn't a part of my life."

One Scripture that he remembers reading while in middle school is Romans 12:1. "Therefore, I urge you, brothers and sisters, in view of God's mercy, to offer your bodies as a living sacrifice, holy and pleasing to God—this is your true and proper worship."

"That Scripture blew me away... letting Christ transform your life and becoming like Him," he said. "Reading scripture and knowing what the Bible said about different situations made Jesus a foundation in my life. There are not many situations the Bible doesn't speak directly to."

Gross continues to grow in his relationship with Jesus. "Everything I do is focused around Christ. I hope my entire time in the Majors represented Him and brought His name to life so others could see Him."

And this is my prayer: that your love may abound more and more in knowledge and depth of insight, so that you may be able to discern what is best and may be pure and blameless for the day of Christ, filled with the fruit of righteousness that comes through Jesus Christ—to the glory and praise of God.

Philippians 1:9-11

"Children are the greatest gift that we have here on earth that God can give us. God compares all of our relationships that we are to have with Him to that of a child because they are so pure and innocent. Children are the greatest example of love, need, desire, innocence and purity that you are going to get."
—Todd Hollandsworth

Todd Hollandsworth

TODD MATHEW HOLLANDSWORTH

BORN: April 20, 1973 in Dayton, OH

FAVORITE BIBLE VERSES: Proverbs 4:18 and the books of Psalm and Proverbs

SAVED: Child

POSITIONS: Outfielder

2011 TEAM: Comcast SportsNet Studio Analyst for the Chicago Cubs

SCHOOL: Newport High School in Bellevue, Washington

DRAFTED: 3rd Round of 1991 draft by Los Angeles Dodgers

DEBUT: April 25, 1995 for Los Angeles Dodgers

SEASONS: 1995 – 2006 (Retired)

TEAMS: Dodgers, Rockies, Cubs, Marlins, Rangers, Braves, Reds, and Indians

NUMBERS: 28, 27, 21, 14, 20, 16

ACCOMPLISHMENTS: National League Rookie of the Year—1996; World Series Champion—2003

The path of righteous is like the first gleam of dawn, shining ever brighter till the full light of day.
—Proverbs 4:18

We are God's children. He has a love so great for us that nothing could ever compare to it. With His love He has created a path for us embraced in righteousness. We cannot earn this righteousness, but we do not have to because our Father in heaven has given it to us. The Lord wants us to do our best to live and love for Him each day.

Years	1995-2006	H	871	SB	75
G	1118	2B	192	CS	43
PA	3492	3B	22	BB	262
AB	3191	HR	98	SO	701
R	451	RBI	401	BA	.273

Righteous

Todd Hollandsworth

THE WORD OF GOD IS "our food and sustenance," said Todd Hollandsworth. Being in the Word every day helps him to think more clearly and to properly understand life. "Everything else starts to make more sense. The greatest wisdom you can obtain is from the Word of God. It's pure unquestionable wisdom and knowledge for everything that you experience on earth. It's the greatest strength you will ever have."

One particular verse that stands out to Hollandsworth in his current walk with Christ is Proverbs 4:18: "The path of the righteous is like the first gleam of dawn, shining ever brighter till the full light of day." He enjoys reading Proverbs because of its knowledge and truthfulness about life.

Being wise in the Word and scripturally sound is what continued to see him through some difficult journeys in life. During his baseball career, Hollandsworth was on top of his game and was named Rookie of the Year in 1996 for the LA Dodgers. Into his first season, however, he broke his hand and his thumb. He never knew what was in store after that. "Looking back, it was a great test of faith—being injured and questioning the future."

"Christ is going to be our backbone. In the Bible there are incredible tests and challenges. It came down to a test of faith," he said. "Are you going to love Jesus on your terms when things are fine and dandy or all the time, knowing there will be challenging and difficult times?"

Hollandsworth realized he was incredibly blessed to be playing the game of baseball and decided he was going to fight until he couldn't fight any more. He did have moments of doubt and weakness and continued to have more injuries later in his career (in the early 2000s). Even when his 11-year career seemed over almost as quickly as it began, he was determined to walk away with a smile on his face ready for the next chapter in life.

"Life is about change. I lived a sheltered life for 25 years. I had to figure out how to coexist in society and that's a challenge," he said. "You realize God has something for you the rest of your life and every last one of us has something next."

For Hollandsworth, God will always be the center of his life followed by his wife and his four children. Although he had a successful career in baseball, his most precious moments were when he got married and when his kids were born. "My wife and I have our problems," he admits. "With four kids there are stresses that knock on the door all the time, but getting back to our roots is what's most important and our roots are in Jesus Christ. Our seeds are deep and we believe we're going to make it no matter what."

Jesus is telling us to maximize life's moments, said Hollandsworth. "There are going to be a lot of opportunities to let our light shine bright. When we get to the end, most of us will ask ourselves 'Did I do enough?' Every one of us should feel like we could have done more."

"There is a bigger purpose and meaning to what I'm doing, and I one hundred percent believe God has called me to baseball."
—Brett Carroll

Brett Carroll

BRETT MICHAEL CARROLL

BORN: October 3, 1982 in Knoxville, TN

FAVORITE BIBLE VERSES: Galatians 2:20, Psalm 37:4, and Colossians 3:23

SAVED: 23 years old

POSITIONS: Outfield

2011 TEAM: Milwaukee Brewers

SCHOOL: Middle Tennessee State University

DRAFTED: 10th Round of 2004 draft by Florida Marlins

DEBUT: June 17, 2007 for Florida Marlins

SEASONS: 2007 – 2011 (Active)

TEAMS: Marlins and Brewers

NUMBER: 25, 15

Delight yourself in the Lord and he will give you the desires of your heart.
—Psalm 37:4

The Lord's love for us is never-ending. He wants us to be happy and to have the desires of our heart. When we surrender our wants to the Lord, He will provide us with everything we need. His desires will become our desires, and we will desire to please the Lord.

The world and its desires pass away, but the man who does the will of God lives forever.
—1 John 2:17

Years	2007-2011	H	58	SB	2
G	175	2B	13	CS	1
PA	322	3B	3	BB	21
AB	286	HR	5	SO	84
R	46	RBI	28	BA	.203

Desire

Brett Carroll

AFTER A LONG TIME OF not reading his Bible, Brett Carroll picked it up six years ago and his life was changed. Psalm 37:4 "Delight yourself in the Lord and he will give you the desires of your heart" was a passage that caught his attention. "It was Him telling me that I've been spending my life running from Him. Things were just enlightened to me. My perspective was different," said Carroll.

Baseball had become Carroll's God. "When I was doing well, I was doing well. When I was doing bad, I was doing bad." He was on a mission to prove his father wrong (who doubted that he'd make it in baseball). "I was playing out of bitterness, and I had a chip on my shoulder. My soul was just dry and empty," Carroll said. "I knew about Jesus, but instead of running to Him with my life and sin, I spent time running from Him."

Now Carroll enjoys reaching out to his teammates and sharing the love of Christ. "I think sometimes we have gotten away from what the Gospel really is and how He reached a lost world," he said. "It's a burden on me to love these guys for where they are at, like God did. Pouring the truth into them brings me a lot of joy."

Doing just that is a lot more exciting than homeruns, he said. "When you start to see lives restored (out of) the brokenness…I'm trying to be a light in the clubhouse."

However, trying to be a light can sometimes be difficult. Other guys will say things under their breath and not want to hear about Jesus. "I want to be real," Carroll said. "Guys see Christians as boring. They don't see that He's created everything. Some have painted a picture that Christians are perfect people. You look in the Bible, and every person has blown it and God continues to restore."

Carroll believes one hundred percent that God has called him to play baseball and to be the hands and feet of Jesus. Revelation 3:8 says "See I have placed before you an open door that no one can shut. I know that you have little strength, yet you have kept my word and have not denied my name." God has opened up many doors for me, said Carroll.

"I think he opened up doors clearly that allowed me to get to the big leagues and that allowed me to use this platform for His glory."

He has had to step back and realize all of these opportunities are a "God thing": such as mission trips to Puerto Rico and Nicaragua he went on with a ministry called UPI. It's been an eye-opening experience for him.

"Baseball is a way of life down there," he explained. "We put on clinics and share the Gospel. It's a way to serve and watch God do some amazing things."

It is still difficult at times for Carroll to wrap his mind around the patience and love of Christ. "It's unbelievable—God's patience with us. People think their salvation is based on what they're doing and not doing. God accepted us the way we are... and (that) flourishes into a life of worship. Before I was born, He knew where I was going to fail and my decisions, and He still lived and died on the cross for us."

Whenever Carroll is signing an autograph, he writes his life verse, Galatians 2:20: "I have been crucified with Christ and I no longer live, but Christ lives in me. The life I live in the body, I live by faith in the Son of God, who loved me and gave himself for me."

Carroll knows the Christian life isn't like a nine-inning game. "It's a lifelong process. It's a journey with the God of the universe who knows you and has perfect plans for you. Why wouldn't I want that?"

"I don't live life for myself anymore. Everything I hopefully try to do has eternal value to it. I am not thinking about myself anymore but thinking about others and how to impact the Kingdom."
—Eddie Taubensee

Eddie Taubensee

EDWARD KENNETH TAUBENSEE

BORN: October 31, 1968 in Beeville, TX
FAVORITE BIBLE VERSES: 1 Corinthians 9:19
SAVED: 1995
POSITIONS: Catcher
2011 TEAM: Director of Baseball Programs for Pro Athletes Outreach
SCHOOL: Maitland High School in Maitland, Florida
DRAFTED: 6th Round of 1986 draft by Cincinnati Reds
DEBUT: May 18, 1991 for Cleveland Indians
SEASONS: 1991 – 2001 (Retired)
TEAMS: Indians, Reds, and Astros
NUMBERS: 56, 6, 10, 16

Though I am free and belong to no man, I make myself a slave to everyone, to win as many as possible.
—1 Corinthians 9:19

Have you ever had the opportunity to help someone out? Maybe it was fixing a flat tire, carrying groceries to a car, or helping around the house. It feels great! This is because the Lord wants us to serve Him and to serve others. Jesus was born to serve us. He did this in the smallest actions of washing feet to the largest action of dying on the cross. We should prepare ourselves for serving others and recognize that each opportunity could be from the Lord.

Years	1991-2001	H	784	SB	11
G	975	2B	151	CS	10
PA	3178	3B	9	BB	255
AB	2874	HR	94	SO	574
R	351	RBI	419	BA	.273

Servant

Eddie Taubensee

EDDIE TAUBENSEE IS USING THE greatest game ever played to tell the greatest story ever told – the story of Jesus Christ. This began in 1995 when he accepted Jesus as his Lord and Savior. "I never went to church or chapel but heard people talk about having a personal relationship with Christ. My idea of that was (that) I can do what I want to do as long as I say some kind of prayer," he said. "I thought that's the way it worked."

Taubensee was drafted and entered the Minor Leagues at the early age of 17. He made it to the Majors five years later. But when he got married, his life began to change. With some resistance, his wife convinced him to attend a Pro Athletes Outreach conference in Orlando, Florida. He just wanted to get in and out of the conference, not expecting to get anything from it.

"The speaker was discussing the Gospel and how God made us in His own image," he said. "I was telling God who I thought He should be instead of who He already is, (wanting) Him to mold to my lifestyle instead of just surrendering to Him. (But) God was working in me. I said 'I give up. I surrender. I've been living a lie and I give it to you.'"

Taubensee began feeling more freedom when he played the game. "I wasn't playing for the fans, or my manager or the media," he said. "I was just playing to honor God and give glory to Him. Whatever the results were, it was out of my hands and all I could do was do my best and play as hard as I could."

Prior to meeting the Lord, Taubensee was a low-key guy who didn't want to ruffle any feathers. "When the Lord took hold of me, there were times I had to stand up for my faith and stand my ground." It was difficult not having much Christian fellowship on the team, but he remained excited about his walk with Christ.

Taubensee tells about how his heart was changed after he met Jesus. It was opening day, April 1, 1996, and Taubensee was the catcher for the Cincinnati Reds playing against the Montreal Expos. He was nervous and talking with the umpire, John McSherry, before the game began. McSherry was jokingly telling him to call all the balls and strikes.

The first inning into the game, McSherry collapsed and died of a heart attack. He was to have been examined that day for arrhythmia, an irregular heart beat, but he had canceled because he didn't want to miss the opening game. "He had a heart condition and knew about it and he waited one day too long," said Taubensee. When speaking with others, he relates that story to those who don't know Jesus.

"It's a spiritual heart condition," he explained. "We just can't wait to take care of it. We have to do something now. You don't know when that time will come. We all have a heart condition we know about, and we need to do something with it."

First Corinthians 9:19 is a verse that stands out for Taubensee: "Though I am free and belong to no man, I make myself a slave to everyone, to win as many as possible."

"I am free in Christ to do whatever I want, but I choose to think about others more than myself," he said. "It's really hard when you're playing baseball to have a servant attitude because all the focus is me, myself and I. It's easy to get caught up in that."

"Coming to Christ didn't mean I was going to all of a sudden hit .300 and be an all-star catcher. All I had was just a cool job. I knew that and knew it was temporary. I embraced it more and enjoyed it more."

Now he's trying to give back to the game of baseball and serves on the board of the Pro Athletes Outreach. Taubensee learns about what is going on in baseball and what issues the players are dealing with. "I'm a generation out," he said. "Ten years ago, we didn't have texting. Now it's such an instant world with the internet, and we need to know how we can impact these players." PAO, Baseball Chapel and Unlimited Potential Inc. are all ministries in baseball that complement each other and work together, he explained.

"God gave me the gift of baseball as a platform," Taubensee said. "I want to use that to share His word and His truth."

Finally, be strong in the Lord and in his mighty power. Put on the full armor of God, so that you can take your stand against the devil's schemes.

Ephesians 6:10-11

"God is preparing me for something. I am not sure what."
—Gary Knotts

Gary Knotts

GARY EVERETT KNOTTS

BORN: February 12, 1977 in Decatur, AL
FAVORITE BIBLE VERSES: Psalm 18:32, Romans 12:1-2, James 1:2-6
SAVED: 16 years old
POSITIONS: Pitcher
2011 TEAM: Pitching Instructor at Integrity Sports Training
www.facebook.com/integritysports
SCHOOL: Brewer High School in Somerville, AL
DRAFTED: 11th Round of 1995 draft by Florida Marlins
DEBUT: July 28, 2001 for Florida Marlins
SEASONS: 2001 – 2004 (Retired)
TEAMS: Marlins and Tigers
NUMBERS: 56, 35

It is God who arms me with strength and makes my way perfect.
—Psalm 18:32

As Christians, we do not need to fear. The Lord is our strength. We are fighting a daily war against Satan in our lives. Jesus has prepared us for this war and has given us the armor we need. Ephesians 6:10-20 speaks of the armor we have been given and how we need to be strong.

Years	2001-2004	L	16	ER	162
G	86	SV	2	HR	41
GS	38	IP	267.1	BB	122
ERA	5.45	H	281	SO	162
W	13	R	172		

Strength

Gary Knotts

ONE OF THE FIRST THINGS Gary Knotts did after getting his drivers license was find a church. At 16 years old, he heard the Word preached when he went to a friend's church. It made sense to him, and he accepted Christ as his Lord and Savior and was hooked. He attended church and took part in Bible studies regularly. "It was the highlight of my life," he said. "The Lord had a calling on my life." Knotts shared the Gospel with his family, and his mother and father received the Lord.

Soon he realized he had a talent for baseball. He continued to pray about the direction his life was taking. "God has proven His sovereignty in my life," he said. "If I wasn't going to get to the big leagues, I was ready to do something else." He joined the Florida Marlins in the 11th round of the 1995 amateur draft and made his Major League pitching debut in 2001.

God helped him through some tough injuries during his career – one of the biggest hurdles for athletes. He was traded to the Detroit Tigers in 2003 but was released two years later due to a shoulder injury that had him out all season. Yet, God continued to show His faithfulness.

"I've had a lot of opportunities to share my faith but I've never been one to push it on anybody," he said. "I've been called to win friends and influence many. I do it by being a man of integrity and a man of my word. I was trying to be a spiritual leader on the team." Knotts said guys would come to him when they were in need of help but had nobody else to turn to. "They would say, 'I know you're a Christian. Will you pray for me?'"

However, Knotts doesn't believe there is a place for evangelists on a baseball team. "You don't want to alienate yourself from the teammates. You want to draw close to them and find something that's a common ground and gain their trust before you can put something heavy on them such as their relationship with God."

"They may not understand the Gospel, but they understand my heart. I know where I'm coming from when I share something of that magnitude and something that's precious to me. That's the way I've lived my life as a ball player," he said. "I believe if I live the way God wants me to, there will be opportunities for me to share."

"I believe God's used me," he added. "I've planted those seeds and God will water them in time."

Knotts has taken part in Home Plate—an event that allows current and past Tigers ball players to share their Christian faith. "It's real neat to see decisions made out of it and the impact being made."

You may call it luck or coincidence, but Knotts has had things, some small and some large, happen in his life that he knows show God was right there with him. There was the time he was having car trouble on the road but the next exit up had the right car dealership that could help him. "That was something that was God's way of saying, 'Look, I'm going to take care of you. Do what I'm calling you to do.' To me it's God taking care of His children."

On a bigger scale, an event that has changed his life happened through the charity World Vision, a Christian humanitarian organization dedicated to working with children, families and their communities. He and his wife, Amanda, help support a little girl from Mexico. They wanted to sponsor a child in honor of his wife's late grandmother Lucille. And their only request was that the girl have the same birthday as Amanda's grandmother.

World Vision didn't have a child with that birthday, but Knotts and his wife received a package in the mail one day with information about a young girl. The girl's name was Lucia—Lucille in English. "That was God saying, 'This is what we're supposed to do,'" said Knotts. "That was a sign from God that we need to support this little girl, whose name means light."

Knotts has no job right now, but has big dreams and big hopes of opening a baseball academy. "If God allows the academy to happen or if He shuts the door, I'll figure something out. The first step is always prayer," he said. "My biggest fault is I want to try and do it on my own, but I need to ask God to do His work and show Himself."

Jesus replied, "If I glorify myself, my glory means nothing. My Father, whom you claim as your God, is the one who glorifies me."

John 8:54

"I have been very blessed to have a professional career and was able to be a part of winning the World Series. I have tried to use that as a platform to glorify God and His Kingdom. A lot of people go through ups and downs and He is the one who pulls us through everything."
—Trot Nixon

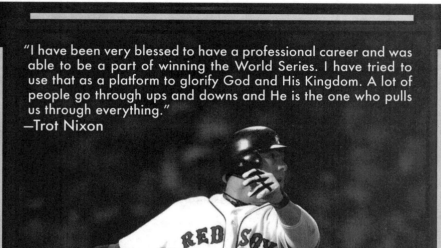

Trot Nixon

CHRISTOPHER TROTMAN NIXON

BORN: April 11, 1974 in Durham, NC
FAVORITE BIBLE VERSES: Psalm 16:8
SAVED: 1993
POSITIONS: Right Field
2011 TEAM: Co-host of "The 5th Quarter" on WWAY News Channel 3
SCHOOL: New Hanover High School in Wilmington, North Carolina
DRAFTED: 1st Round of 1993 draft by Boston Red Sox
DEBUT: September 21, 1996 for Boston Red Sox
SEASONS: 1996 – 2008 (Retired)
TEAMS: Red Sox, Indians, and Mets
NUMBERS: 7, 33, 6
ACCOMPLISHMENTS: World Series Champion—2004

I have set the Lord always before me. Because he is at my right hand, I will not be shaken.
—Psalm 16:8

All our successes in life can be contributed to our Heavenly Father. Jesus is at the Father's right hand and keeps us from being shaken. We should remember that each day is a blessing from the Lord and ask Him to help us glorify Him with all that we do. When we choose to serve the Lord and let our actions speak for Jesus, we impact the lives of those around us.

Years	1996-2008	H	995	SB	30
G	1092	2B	222	CS	13
PA	4224	3B	28	BB	504
AB	3627	HR	137	SO	689
R	579	RBI	555	BA	.274

Glorify

Trot Nixon

TROT NIXON AND HIS TEAM, the Boston Red Sox, won the World Series in 2004. He had worked his entire baseball career for this moment, but Nixon wasn't as excited as he should be. "I realized I obtained the mountaintop," he said. "I put this World Series on my mountaintop."

Christ opened his eyes that night as he sat in his apartment watching the event replayed on television. "I felt the emptiness in my stomach. I realized Christ needed to be my mountaintop. Now He's on my pedestal because I'm always trying to reach Him and working toward Him," Nixon said. "God was saying, 'Use this opportunity to glorify me.'"

While playing ball, Nixon had Psalm 16:8 stitched into his glove. "I keep my eyes always on the Lord. Sometimes you're in the batter's box and facing the greatest closers of all time and (I remember) God's at my right hand and I will not be shaken," he said. "There are a lot of things that worry people in their lives—that scare them. God has His hand in everything."

Nixon accepted Christ in 1993 when he had just started playing professional baseball. When he reached the Major Leagues, he was able to learn more about the Bible. Walt Day, a chaplain with Athletes in Action, broke it down and answered his questions. Nixon learned how awesome Jesus really is! Nixon received a copy of the NIV version of the Bible and loved it. "I was interested in reading about Jesus' life."

"I'm thankful to live in a country that allows me to learn about Him and voice my opinions about Him," he said. "It's pretty simple.

Most kid's blessing at the table is 'God is great. God is good.' We need to take that opportunity and open our eyes every single day to see how good He is and how great He is."

Although he knows he'll face spiritual warfare in everything he does, Nixon is keeping Christ on his pedestal and is working toward Him. Whether in speaking engagements or going on future mission trips to the Czech Republic or elsewhere to teach others about baseball and Christ, he stays focused.

"The only fulfillment you're going to have in life is having a personal relationship with Christ and Christ being on that mountaintop."

"We are all there at some time in our walk. We come to a crossroads and we must decide what we believe."
—Todd Jones

Todd Jones

TODD BARTON GIVIN JONES

BORN: April 24, 1968 in Marietta, GA

FAVORITE BIBLE VERSES: John 20:29

SAVED: October 6, 1991

POSITIONS: Pitcher

SCHOOL: Jacksonville State University

DRAFTED: 1st Round of 1989 draft by Houston Astros

DEBUT: July 7, 1993 for Houston Astros

SEASONS: 1993 – 2008 (Retired)

TEAMS: Astros, Tigers, Twins, Rockies, Red Sox, Reds, Phillies and Marlins

NUMBERS: 56, 35

ACCOMPLISHMENTS: All Star Selection—2000; American League Rolaids Relief Man of the Year—2000

Then Jesus told him, "Because you have seen me, you have believed; blessed are those who have not seen and yet have believed."
—John 20:29

We have a decision to make in our lives. Do we believe in Jesus Christ as our Lord and Savior or not? Jesus wants to change our lives and direct us toward Him. Sometimes it is hard for us to have faith in what we cannot see. However, the Lord promises that He will bless us if we believe in Him although we have not physically seen Him. If you look into His blessings, you will see Him.

Years	1993-2003	L	63	ER	473
G	982	SV	319	HR	93
GS	1	IP	1072.0	BB	443
ERA	3.97	H	1072	SO	868
W	58	R	518		

Changed

MEETING A YOUNG BOY WHO was the victim of a spinal cord injury helped remind Todd Jones to get back up and try again. Jones was having a rough time playing for the Rockies in 2003. "I get home that winter and I think I'm finished," he said. "I had my ten years in and some cash in the bank. I was okay with how my career had gone, but I knew I didn't want to go through getting hit hard again. Then I met a guy in my hometown who changed my perspective."

John Paul Montgomery was a football player on the local high school team when he got injured. "He was a great kid that got handed a bad break, but his spirit was happy, full of joy and positive," Jones said. He watched him struggle each day, and it stirred something inside Jones.

Jones and other volunteers helped build a wheelchair-accessible home for the Montgomery family by using Jones' salary from the following season. "God calls us to pick up His cross and follow Him daily. I was going to stop playing because I had a bad year? I felt like I was commanded by God to get off my tushy and help somebody out. I was obedient, and God was glorified through that whole process. God teaches us that it's okay to get knocked down, but it's not okay to not get back up and try again." And that's what Jones did. He played five more years and retired after the 2008 season.

Although Jones came to know Christ as a young boy, he called it more a matter of "fire insurance." It wasn't until later that he rededicated his life and was baptized in 1991. "I went to church and pulled Christ out of my back pocket on Wednesday and Sunday, but I didn't let Jesus be Lord of my life until 2003," he said. "I had a total transformation, and since then I have tried to use Biblical life application daily."

"We come to a crossroads and we must decide what we believe," said Jones. "Are we going to be committed to serving Christ and allow Him to be a part of our life and include us in His master plan or are we going to fight Him and do things on our own?"

Jones says that Christians are going to mess up regularly, but we are still called to follow Jesus. We can't handle life on our own. "The Lord has helped me through trying times in many ways," he said. "Like the stories we read in the Bible from Noah to Moses and David to Saul. If we let Jesus change us He will."

He feels that his walk with Christ has been transformed since helping Montgomery. "All I want to do is tell people about Jesus; not with words but with actions and helping out where I can and being a good steward of what's been given to me." He believes that time is running out. "We have to tell as many people as we can the good news. If we'll hurry up and do our job, then we can get to heaven faster."

"If God hadn't put on me (that I should run), I would have missed out on a lot of beautiful experiences. That's how much He looks after me and how much my Father loves me."
-Trever Miller

Trever Miller

TREVER DOUGLAS MILLER

Born: May 29, 1973 in Louisville, KY
Favorite Bible Verses: Daily Reading
Confirmed: 8 years old
Positions: Pitcher
2011 Teams: St. Louis Cardinals, Toronto Blue Jays, and
Boston Red Sox
School: Trinity High School in Louisville, KY
Drafted: 1st Round of 1991 draft by Detroit Tigers
Debut: September 4, 1996 for Detroit Tigers
Seasons: 1996 – 2011 (Active)
Teams: Tigers, Astros, Phillies, Dodgers, Devil Rays, Rays, Cardinals,
Blue Jays, and Red Sox
Number: 37, 46, 51, 47, 57, 43, 56

*Blessed is the man who perseveres under trial, because when he has
stood the test, he will receive the crown of life that God has promised
to those who love him.*
–James 1:12

There are times of trial and challenges in our lives that can feel over-
whelming. By surrendering to the Lord and keeping faith in Jesus we
will persevere. Through this perseverance the Lord blesses us. Matthew
5 speaks of those who the Lord blesses.

Years	1996-2011	L	17	ER	243
G	694	SV	11	HR	54
GS	5	IP	523.1	BB	237
ERA	4.18	H	521	SO	434
W	18	R	264		

Blessed

Trever Miller

TREVER MILLER'S FAITH IN THE Lord has had its ups and downs—from his baseball-related injuries to his daughter's rare chromosomal disorder. But Miller has never fully turned his back on God. "My personal belief is if you don't have God in your life, He will give you something you can't handle," he explains. "If you do have Him in your life, whatever He gives you, you can handle."

During Miller's first Spring Training game, he suffered a devastating injury that almost took his life. A line drive slammed into his face, breaking his cheekbones and a sinus cavity. "The Lord and His 10,000 angels were looking out for me that day," he said. "I could have died."

He credits his faith with helping him understand it was a freak accident and giving him the courage to get back on the field after healing. "It was a blow to my confidence. Without my strong Catholic faith and knowing who to turn to in that situation, I probably wouldn't have made it through. I would have healed up, but I doubt I would have gotten back out," he said. "My faith in Him allowed me to overcome the fear of the ball and to trust my hands again."

Although he's had some career challenges, his biggest one is in his role as a father to Grace, who was born with two holes in her heart and a rare genetic disorder that doesn't even have a name. The prognosis was grim. In fact, doctors suggested they let Grace slowly pass away. But the Millers made sure Grace had a fighting chance.

"We couldn't (let her pass)," Miller said. "My faith will not allow that. It was not up to us. We were going to do everything we could to provide for her." Grace wasn't supposed to live past her first birthday, but now she's 7 years old. She is the first child to live longer than one year with this disorder.

"She's the biggest blessing I've ever received from my Lord and Savior," he said. "It is challenging. I explain to dads who are true family men… they get it as a man, father and husband you want to be able to fix it: like a chain on a bike, the car…anything that's broken and put food on the table. But in this situation there was nothing I could do. I was helpless."

It was then that Miller began rebelling against God. With the hospital visits and never knowing what the next day might hold, one day in frustration he threw his Bible against the wall and walked out to go on his next road trip. His wife, who always tucked his Bible into his bag so he could sit and pray while traveling, picked up the Bible and snuck it in the bag. "When I got to the hotel and settled in, I opened up my bag and there it was. That's how strong she is in her personal faith and walk with Christ and how much she leaned on the Lord."

Miller said he definitely doesn't understand everything that goes on in his life. But he's learned one thing: "His will be done. It's better for me to just keep quiet and do His will and let Him lead. But that's very difficult sometimes. You want to take over, but that's always a bad move."

He realizes how tough it is to be a Christian in today's world with the growing influence of social media and temptations every-where. "The world is growing in sin and it's difficult to navigate that. It's not possible to navigate it without God and having Christian faith." Miller adds that he doesn't envy his children's generation because they probably have the toughest walk in faith of any gen-eration. "The world they are living in is so sensational, (with prayer taken) out of schools and faith and religion being attacked."

Parents, Miller believes, have to be the guiding force: "Take care of your house, expand from there and be a role model to these kids. (They need to) see us on bended knee praying at the dinner table and standing hand-in-hand at church worshipping God so they know there is a greater power out there. It's not the television, Blackberry, iPhone or iPad. That stuff will perish and fade away, but God will always be there."

Miller knows he's been extremely blessed by the Lord to be given the talent to play ball for more than eleven years in the big leagues. "I've never taken it for granted, which is why I remain in the game," he explained. "There are kids out there that enjoy what I do and look up to me. That's a massive responsibility I don't take lightly."

He remembers a time he became overwhelmed by his daughter's daily care. He let his frustrations get the best of him and bought a 6-pack of beer after a tough game. As he sat by the swimming pool, the rain poured down on him. He was mad at the world–and mad at God. After he woke up the next morning, he felt the Lord was telling him to go for a jog and release his frustrations. He found an old pair of running shoes and threw them on. "I struggled in the hot Florida sun, but when I was finished I felt better," Miller said.

Running has become an important part of his life. He usually heads to the ballpark before a game and runs laps. He also participates in races. One run was especially memorable. For the Turkey Trot 10k in Clearwater, Florida he was able to push Grace [in a running stroller] with him. This will be his sixth year participating. Running a marathon was the next step. He wanted to do it in honor of Grace. He completed it and put the medal around his little girl's neck. "It became my passion," he said. Miller also has two other children, so he decided that he'd better run two more to present them with medals as well. He ran Disney Marathons and did just that.

Now he hosts the Trever Miller Mob 5k/1 mile race in Florida. All proceeds benefit the Kiwanis of Gulf Beaches Miracle League, a non-profit committed to helping children with disabilities have the chance to play baseball.

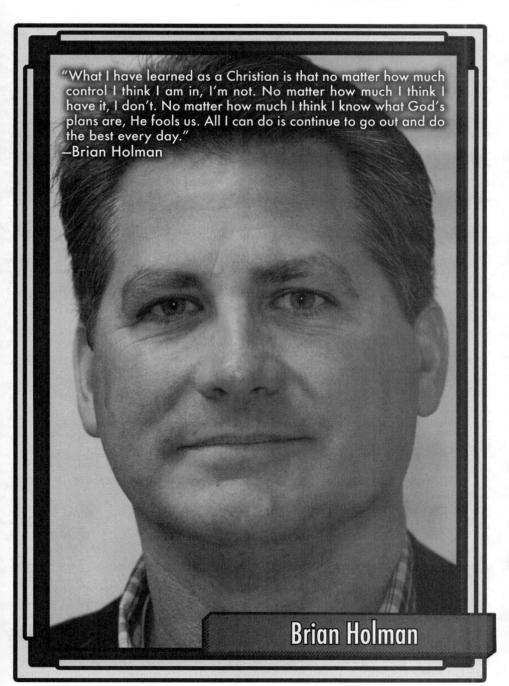

"What I have learned as a Christian is that no matter how much control I think I am in, I'm not. No matter how much I think I have it, I don't. No matter how much I think I know what God's plans are, He fools us. All I can do is continue to go out and do the best every day."
—Brian Holman

Brian Holman

BRIAN SCOTT HOLMAN

BORN: January 25, 1965 in Denver, CO

FAVORITE BIBLE VERSES: Colossians 3:23

SAVED: October 31, 1988

POSITIONS: Pitcher

2011 TEAM: Managing Director of Ronald Blue & Co., LLC and Pitching Instructor at Brian Holman Baseball www.brianholmanbaseball.com

SCHOOL: North Wichita, Kansas High School

DRAFTED: 1st Round of 1983 draft by Montreal Expos

DEBUT: June 25, 1988 for Montreal Expos

SEASONS: 1988-1991 (Retired)

TEAMS: Expos and Mariners

NUMBERS: 59, 36

Whatever you do, work at it with all your heart, as working for the Lord, not for men.
—Colossians 3:23

We want to be able to do as we please and to control the outcome of everything that we do. This often translates into not wanting to pay the penalty for something we decided to do even though we knew that it was wrong. We do not need to have control of the outcome because the Lord has His plans for us. What we need to understand is that we must seize each day for the Lord and give all we have. We can take heart knowing that Jesus is completely in control.

Years	1988-1991	L	45	ER	279
G	109	SV	0	HR	47
GS	99	IP	676.2	BB	254
ERA	3.71	H	682	SO	392
W	37	R	303		

Heart

Brian Holman

AN ALCOHOLIC FAMILY, A TROUBLED marriage and sick children could have torn Brian Holman's life apart, but after accepting the Lord into his heart he learned how to get through the trials of life.

Many of us tend to say, "This isn't fair" or "Why me?" when we are experiencing a challenge in our lives. "Everything that goes on—you know there is an eternal perspective that you can't see," Holman said. "Maybe God is allowing something to happen to strengthen you or help others. We don't know why, and there is no rhyme or reason."

Growing up with an alcoholic father caused heartache for Holman. They often had no money and would be evicted from their home or have their electricity cut off. Holman's father dealt with the stress of his financial problems by drinking. "I would go to work with him in the summers. He would get drunk, and I would have to drive the car home in order to get to my baseball games," he said. "There I was, fourteen, driving across Denver in rush-hour traffic. It created a lot of anger, anxiety and frustration. When I got to the baseball field, I would want to kill the other team."

Holman's past had a big impact on his future. "Baseball was my saving grace growing up." After his senior year, he was drafted by the Montreal Expos in the first round. Three years into his Minor League baseball career, he met his wife Jami.

He admits he was close to getting a divorce at one point in his marriage as he and his wife dealt with their difficult backgrounds. Holman continued to hold onto the belief that everything would be fine once he made it to the big leagues. But he continued to be disappointed and frustrated. Things began to change shortly after Jami accepted Christ as her Lord and Savior.

"About a month after Jami came to the Lord, she had a Bible study at our home in Montreal and asked if I wanted to join her," he said. "I started to leave and something said to stay and listen." Not walking through that door changed his life forever.

"I hammered them about God and the lady leading the Bible study backed everything up with Scripture and explained it," said Holman. "This light bulb went off, and I thought 'Oh my God, this is true.'" Holman accepted Christ on October 31, 1988, and his life was dramatically changed.

"I didn't know anything about what being saved was," he added. "You get this belief that everything is going to be fine now. God works in the midst of difficulties. The only way I believe I've been able to overcome so many things is because of the relationship I have with God."

"I used to get caught up in... Why did this happen? Why didn't I get to play baseball and make millions? Why did my son have a brain tumor? Why did my daughter have leukemia?" Holman said. "The bottom line is Christians are not exempt from trials. Jesus said in this world you will have them, but He also said 'Have no fear because I have overcome the world.'"

Holman is now a financial advisor with Ronald Blue & Co., a financial services firm based on Biblical principles of money and finance. "Because of what I've gone through, it helps me talk to clients. I remind them that there are problems that money can fix, and then there are *real* problems. I've been doing things with the Lord for many years now. He's been faithful through it all."

"Live life and try to honor and serve the Lord," is what he lives by. "One day I'll stand before Him, and He'll say, 'Remember all of those things you went through? This is why.' It takes a lot of frustration off of me."

"You find your way through these nine innings of life and come out on the other end doing the best you could." He adds, "And the Lord will say, 'Well done, good and faithful servant.'"

Invitation

IF YOU HAVE NOT SURRENDERED your life to Jesus Christ and asked Him to be your Lord and Savior, I pray that you will right now. Asking Jesus to be my Lord and Savior has been the most important decision I have ever made. I personally have experienced the power of Jesus in my life and am excited about having eternal life with Him.

Romans 10:9 states, "If you confess with your mouth, 'Jesus is Lord,' and believe in your heart that God raised him from the dead, you will be saved."

The way we surrender our lives to the Lord is through believing in Him. We show this belief by praying and asking Him to take control of our lives. If you would like to ask Jesus into your life, please pray the following prayer:

Dear Lord Jesus,

I pray to You knowing that I am a sinner and that the only way to eternal life is through You, Jesus. I believe that You died on the cross and rose from the dead and that You ascended into heaven to save me of my sins. I pray that You come into my life, take full control and save me from my sins. I surrender my all to You, and I trust You to be my personal Lord and Savior. I pray that Your will be done in my life. Thank you, Jesus, for loving me, for saving me, and for giving me eternal life with You. In Your name I pray. - Amen

If you prayed this prayer to accept Jesus as your Lord and Savior, then I am excited for you! Right now you are probably wondering what to do next. I recommend telling a friend. I also recommend getting plugged into a church and reading the Holy Bible daily.

If you are trying to find a church, I invite you to visit mine, NewSpring Church in South Carolina. We have campuses in several cities as well as an online campus at www.newspring.cc.

God Bless,
Kevin Morrisey

Foundation Information

JESUS TOLD US TO GO to all ends of the world to spread the word about Christ. There are several Christian organizations that minister to Major League Baseball players and their families. The players have an opportunity to stay plugged into the Word of God and spend time with other believers through these groups. Three of the organizations are Baseball Chapel, Pro Athletes Outreach, and Unlimited Potential Incorporated.

- Baseball Chapel – *www.baseballchapel.org*
- Pro Athletes Outreach – *www.pao.org*
- Unlimited Potential Incorporated – *www.upi.org*

Baseball players volunteer and donate their time, finances, and gifts to help many organizations. Many of them are faith-based sports groups that minister to athletes of all ages. Several of the players mentioned a few of the groups they support.

- Athletes in Action – *www.athletesinaction.org*
- Baseball Country – *www.baseballcountry.com*
- Fellowship of Christian Athletes – *www.fca.org*
- Hockey Ministries International – *www.hockeyministries.org*
- Purpose Driven Baseball – *www.purposedrivenbaseball.com*
- Teammates For Kids – *www.teammatesforkids.com*

Many of the players are active in community organizations. Several of these organizations are faith-based. They all reach out to communities internationally or locally.

- Alongside Her – *www.alongsideher.org*
- Diaz Family Foundation – *www.diazfamilyfoundation.org*
- Donate Life – www.donatelife.net
- Honoring The Father – www.honoringthefather.com
- Mailbox Club – www.mailboxclub.org
- Miracle League of Gulf Beaches – www.miracleleaguegulfbeaches.com
- The Jesus Film Project – www.jesusfilm.org
- Tim Salmon Foundation – www.timsalmon.com
- World Vision International – www.wvi.org

Source Notes

Baseball Players Statistics and Playing History
Baseball-Reference.com. Last updated 2 November 2010. On-line.
24 March 2011.
Sports Reference LLC., 2000–2011.
Available WWW: http://www.baseball-reference.com/

Player Photo Reference
Andy Phillips, by Keith Allison
Ben Zobrist, provided by the Tampa Bay Rays
Brian Holman, provided by Brian Holman
Brett Carroll, provided by Brett Carroll
Britt Reames, by Kevin Morrisey
Bryan Hickerson, provided by Bryan Hickerson
Eddie Taubensee, provided by Eddie Taubensee
Jose Alvarez, provided by Jose Alvarez
Landon Powell, provided by Landon Powell
Matt Diaz, provided by the Diaz Family Foundation
Gabe Gross, provided by the Tampa Bay Rays
Gary Knotts, provided by Home Plate Detroit
Greg McMichael, provided by Greg McMichael
Ricky Horton, provided by Ricky Horton
Scott Sanderson, provided by Moye Sports
Stephen Drew, by John Telleria
Steve Foster, provided by Steve Foster

Steve Sisco, provided by Steve Sisco
Tim Burke, provided by Tim Burke
Tim Drew, provided by Tim Drew
Tim Salmon, by US Army Photo/Sgt. Jessica R. Dahlberg
Todd Jones, by Kelly McNair
Todd Hollandsworth, by Debbie Lee
Todd Worrell, by Dolores Ford Mobley
Trever Miller, provided by Trever Miller
Trot Nixon, provided by the Boston Red Sox

For more information about
Kevin Morrisey
&
Elizabeth Morrisey
please visit:

www.kevin-morrisey.com
www.lizmorrisey.com
www.facebook.com/Godslineup

For more information about
AMBASSADOR INTERNATIONAL
please visit:

www.ambassador-international.com
@AmbassadorIntl
www.facebook.com/AmbassadorIntl